USDA

United States
Department of
Agriculture

Forest
Service

Northern
Research Station

General Technical
Report NRS-7

AFTER THE BLOWDOWN: A RESOURCE ASSESSMENT OF THE BOUNDARY WATERS CANOE AREA WILDERNESS, 1999 - 2003

W. Keith Moser, Mark H. Hansen, Mark D. Nelson, Susan J. Crocker,
Charles H. Perry, Bethany Schulz, Christopher W. Woodall,
Linda M. Nagel, Manfred E. Mielke

Abstract

The Boundary Waters Canoe Area Wilderness (BWCAW) is an ecological and recreational treasure situated within the Superior National Forest in northern Minnesota, USA. It contains some of the last unspoiled remnants of the great North Woods of the Lake Superior region. A major storm hit the BWCAW on July 4, 1999. Known as the "Boundary Waters-Canadian Derecho," this rare type of storm lasted for more than 22 hours, traveled more than 1,300 miles, and produced wind speeds averaging almost 60 mph. Following the devastation of the windstorm, the Forest Inventory and Analysis unit of the Northern Research Station collaborated with the Eastern Region of the USDA Forest Service and the Minnesota Department of Natural Resources to sample this landscape and assess the effects of this catastrophic event.

Live-tree volume per acre estimates in the BWCAW were 29 percent lower for plots damaged by wind (796 cubic feet/acre) than for plots with no disturbance (1,128 cubic feet/acre). For the aspen/birch forest-type group and the hardwoods supergroup, volume per acre was significantly lower in blowdown conditions than in conditions of no disturbance. Mean fuel loadings estimates indicate that blowdown areas had nearly twice the 100- and 1,000-hr+ fuels as the non-blowdown areas. The means of 10-, 100-, and 1,000-hr+ fuel loadings in BWCAW blowdown areas were higher than the means for these three classes in the BWCAW non-blowdown areas.

Almost every comparison between forest types showed a decline in overstory species diversity in blowdown areas compared to non-blowdown areas. Only aspen and other hardwoods and nonstocked forest-type groups showed a negligible change. When we examined understory diversity, measured by species richness, we found just the opposite: most of the blowdown sites showed increased diversity. The exceptions to this trend were in paper birch and balsam fir forest types.

Northern Research Station

U.S. Department of Agriculture – Forest Service

11 Campus Boulevard Suite 200

Newtown Square, PA 19073-3294

2007

www.nrs.fs.fed.us

AFTER THE BLOWDOWN: A RESOURCE ASSESSMENT OF THE BOUNDARY WATERS CANOE AREA WILDERNESS, 1999 - 2003

W. Keith Moser, Mark H. Hansen, Mark D. Nelson, Susan J. Crocker,
Charles H. Perry, Bethany Schulz, Christopher W. Woodall,
Linda M. Nagel, Manfred E. Mielke

USDA Forest Service

Forest Inventory and Analysis, Northern Research Station, and

Northeastern Area, State and Private Forestry, St. Paul, Minnesota

Acknowledgments

This study would not have been possible without the support of the Superior National Forest; Northeastern Area, State and Private Forestry; and the Minnesota Department of Natural Resources. Some maps were provided by Dale Gormanson and Barry T. Wilson.

Photographs are courtesy of Dave Hansen, University of Minnesota Agricultural Experiment Station.

FOREWORD

The Boundary Waters Canoe Area Wilderness (BWCAW) is an ecological and recreational treasure within the Superior National Forest (SNF) in northern Minnesota that is comprised of a patchwork of lakes and forests. Portions of the BWCAW and neighboring Quetico Provincial Park in Ontario, Canada, contain some of the last unspoiled remnants of the great North Woods of the Lake Superior region. A resource assessment of the BWCAW presented both a challenge and an opportunity for the Northern Research Station's Forest Inventory and Analysis (NRS FIA) program. This program was originally designed to provide strategic inventories of the forest resources for all 50 states. NRS FIA's strength lies in its grid-based plot system, which provides accurate estimates over large areas, e.g., states.

Following the devastating windstorm in July 1999, there was a need to inventory the BWACW. NRS FIA collaborated with the Eastern Region of the USDA Forest Service and the Minnesota Department of Natural Resources to meet the challenge of sampling this landscape and assessing the effects of that catastrophe. The SNF funded a temporary intensification of NRS FIA's sampling scheme, allowing the collection of more data in the BWCAW than otherwise would have been possible. The goals of this report are to summarize some of the data collected and examine the impact of the windstorm on the BWCAW. The Forest Service's Northeastern Area, State and Private Forestry provided funding for this report, which is a collaborative effort of the National Forest System, State and Private Forestry, NRS FIA, and the Minnesota Department of Natural Resources.

CONTENTS

The Boundary Waters Canoe Area Wilderness

Embedded in the Quetico-Superior region of northeastern Minnesota and south-western Ontario, Canada, the Boundary Waters Canoe Area Wilderness (BWCAW) spans 1.1 million acres of the Superior National Forest (SNF) (Fig. 1). Forests and lakes form the predominant land cover of the BWCAW (Fig. 2). Numerous factors, including topography, species mix, and history (managed and unmanaged), and individual disturbances such as fire, weather, and animal browsing have shaped BWCAW's forests. The result is a mosaic of vegetation structures, species, and ages.

Figure 1. The Boundary Waters Canoe Area Wilderness, Superior National Forest in Minnesota.

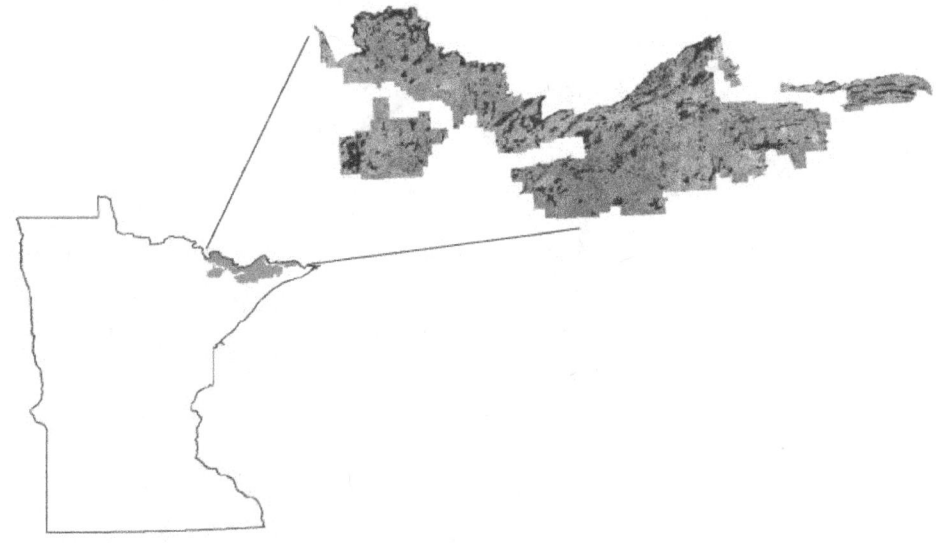

Figure 2. Land cover within the Boundary Waters Canoe Area Wilderness (U.S. Geological Survey, National Land Cover Dataset of 2001).

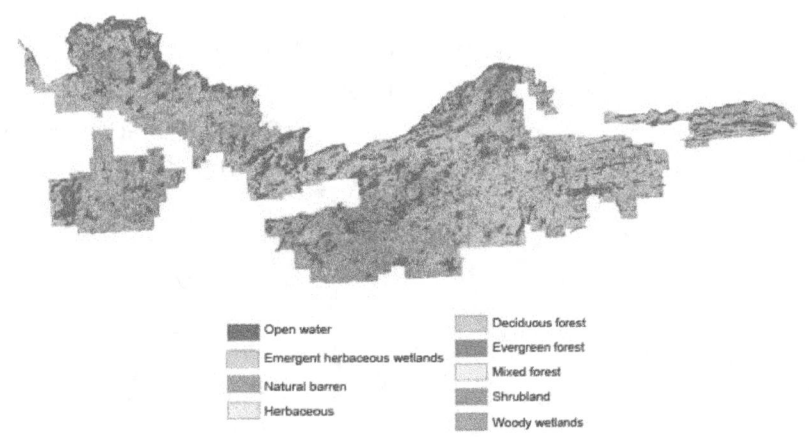

Open water
Emergent herbaceous wetlands
Natural barren
Herbaceous

Deciduous forest
Evergreen forest
Mixed forest
Shrubland
Woody wetlands

Located on the southern portion of the Canadian Shield, the BWCAW was shaped by glaciers that exposed bedrock and formed a multitude of lakes connected by streams and later by portages. Controlled first by the Sioux and later by the Ojibwe peoples, the Boundary Waters area was occupied by the French, British and, after the Louisiana Purchase in 1803, the Americans. Two treaties, the first with the British in 1842 that fixed the boundary between the United States and Canada and the second between the United States and the western Ojibwe in 1854, opened the region to exploration and settlement. There was some interest in gold mining but the real mineral wealth lay in various iron ores in the ground, resulting in extensive open-pit and deep-shaft mining activity which, in turn, led to the establishment of numerous settlements (Heinselman 1996).

By World War I, much of the land in the present BWCAW had been burned or logged. As a result, white pine, red pine, and white spruce declined in dominance while aspen, jack pine, balsam fir, and black spruce became more prominent. As people became more interested in using the region's wildlands for recreation and in exploiting its resources, conservation became a popular cause among many Minnesotans, resulting in successive withdrawals of land from management and development and the designation of much of it as the Superior National Forest in 1909 (Heinselman 1996). The strip of border country from Basswood Lake to Saganaga Lake, which contains some of the most ecologically interesting portions of the present BWCAW, was added to the Forest in 1936. Many administrative and policy initiatives affected the region in the intervening years, but the most significant was the Wilderness Act of 1964, which designated the BWCAW as a unit of the National Wilderness Preservation System. This act recognized the "unique history and character" of the BWCAW and provided for special management considerations that have shaped the Boundary Waters to this day (Heinselman 1973).

Today, the BWCAW is one of the most popular wilderness areas in the country, receiving hundreds of thousands of visitors each year. Lacking roads and motorized vehicles, most of the BWCAW is accessible only by foot, canoe, or kayak. With more than 1,500 miles of waterway, it is a popular backcountry destination (USDA Forest Service 2006).

On July 4, 1999, a major storm event within the BWCAW, known as the Boundary Waters-Canadian Derecho, lasted for more than 22 hours, traveled more than 1,300 miles, and produced windspeeds averaging nearly 60 mph. The blowdown caused widespread devastation with casualties both in Canada and the United States. Moving from WSW to ENE, the storm entered the Arrowhead region of northeastern Minnesota in the early afternoon. Here, winds of 80 to 100 mph resulted in injuries to about 60 canoe campers and damage to tens of millions of trees within 477,000 acres of forest land on the SNF (USDA Forest Service 2002) in the course of leveling a swath 30 miles long and 4 to 12 miles wide. Such a storm can dramatically affect water quality, increase the potential for wildfire, and significantly influence forest composition. It was because of the latter that the Northern Research Station's Forest Inventory and Analysis (NRS FIA) program was requested to intensify the sample of its inventory within the BWCAW.

How Much was Standing: Standing Volume After the Blowdown

How We Estimated It NRS FIA field plot data were combined with geospatial datasets in a geographic information system to estimate the net cubic-foot volume of all live trees on forest land in the SNF, in BWCAW, in blowdown polygons, and within a 3-mile buffer surrounding the blowdown polygons (Fig. 3). Estimates were further stratified by field-level observations of plot-condition attributes, including softwoods vs. hardwoods, forest type, forest-type group, and disturbance codes (Table 1). Variances of these volume estimates, calculated under the assumption of simple random sampling, were used to determine 90-percent confidence intervals. Paired comparisons of estimates, e.g., inside vs. outside blowdown polygons, were interpreted as being significantly different when their respective confidence intervals were not overlapping.

Figure 3. Superior National Forest, Boundary Waters Canoe Area Wilderness, and blowdown areas, St. Louis, Lake, and Cook Counties, Minnesota.

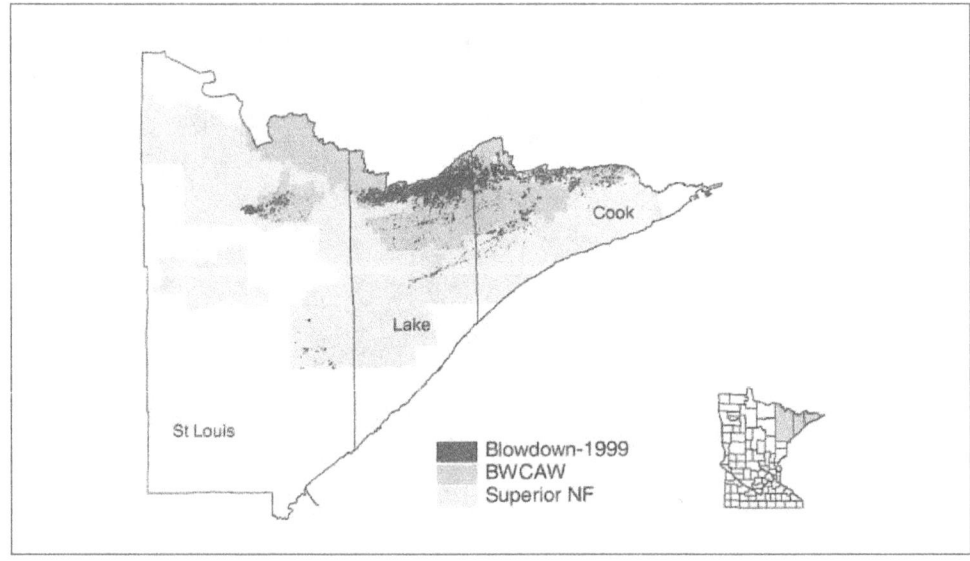

Table 1. Categories for estimating forest volume.

Attribute	Source	Description
County	Geographic	St. Louis, Lake, Cook – political boundaries
SNF	Geographic	Superior National Forest – administrative boundary
BWCAW	Geographic	Boundary Waters Canoe Area Wilderness – administrative boundary
Blowdown	Geographic	Polygon delineation of blowdown area classified via LandsatTM imagery
5-km (3-mile) buffer	Geographic	Area encompassed by 5-km (3-mile) buffer surrounding blowdown polygons
Forest type	Plot	Jack pine type, aspen type
Forest-type group	Plot	White/red/jack pine group, aspen/birch group
Forest super group	Plot	Softwoods, hardwoods
Disturbance code	Plot	None (0), Unknown/not sure (70), Wind or weather (50 or 52), Other

What We Found

Estimates of net cubic-foot (ft^3) volume per acre of all live trees on forest land did not differ significantly between the BWCAW (1,066 ft^3/acre) and the remainder of SNF outside the BWCAW (990 ft^3/acre) (Fig. 4). Likewise, volume estimates within forest-type groups and forest types were not significantly different between BWCAW and non-BWCAW portions of the SNF.

Figure 4. Forest volume within the Superior National Forest inside vs. outside the Boundary Waters Canoe Area Wilderness.

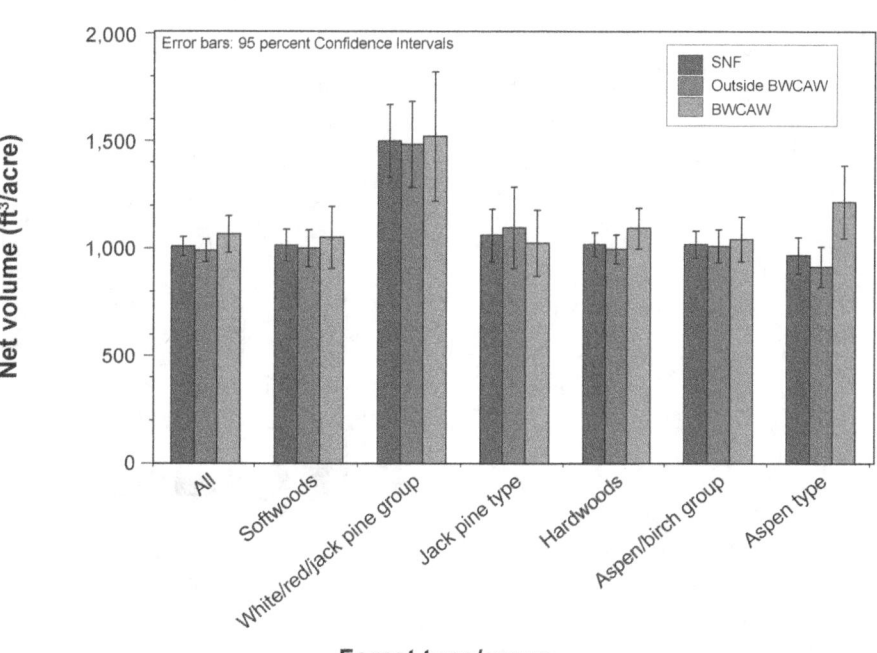

Within the 3-mile buffer area of the BWCAW (Fig. 5), estimates of volume per acre were significantly lower for forest land with condition-level plot observations of wind damage than for undisturbed forest land, for all types/groups (707 vs. 1,154 ft³/acre), softwoods (582 vs. 1,003 ft³/acre), hardwoods (763 vs. 1,322 ft³/acre), and aspen/birch group (748 vs. 1,282 ft³/acre). Again, there were too few NRS FIA plots from other forest-type groups for comparisons of volume by condition damage code within the 3-mile buffer.

Figure 5. Forest volume within Boundary Waters Canoe Area Wilderness, inside a 3-mile (5 km) buffer surrounding and including blowdown polygons.

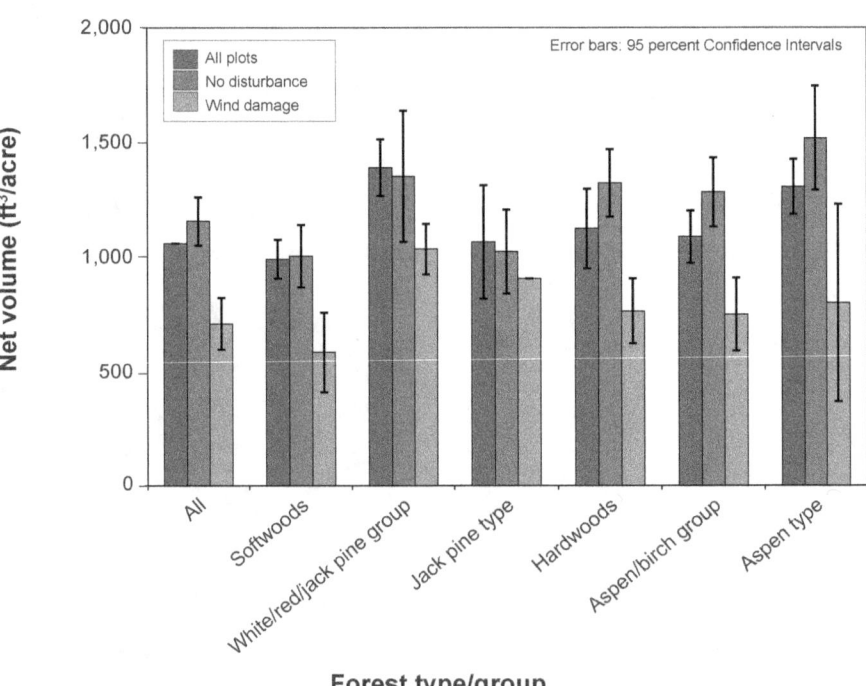

What This Means
Forest volume per acre did not differ significantly between the BWCAW and the remainder of SNF. Therefore, per-acre volume of trees for all forest types was the same inside the BWCAW as it was in the Superior National Forest, but outside of the BWCAW. Looking just at forest land within the BWCAW, standing volume on forest land within the blowdown was significantly lower than that outside the blowdown. While this was expected, it is interesting that not all blowdown plots were void of standing trees, nor was it consistent across forest types. This was due to different levels of wind damage across the landscape and differences in susceptibility to damage among forest types. Although both plot-level FIA data and remote sensing-based geospatial data were useful for comparing blowdown and non-blowdown forest volume, we favored a hybrid approach, using geospatial data to focus analyses on the vicinity of blowdown damage, coupled with analysis of FIA inventory data based on field observations of wind damage.

How Much was Blown Down: NRS FIA Assessment of Down Woody Material

The BWCAW blowdown had substantial impacts on fuel and stand attributes at various spatial scales (Mattson and Shriner 2001). The amount of fuel in the BWCAW was increased substantially. This has increased the probability of wildfire within or adjacent to the wilderness (Leuschen et al. 2000). It is estimated that the range in total woody fuel loadings increased from 4 to 20 tons/acre to 45 to 100 tons/acre as a result of the blowdown. The estimated mean fuel loading in a typical BWCAW stand is 10 tons/acre (Leuschen et al. 2000). Assessing the down woody fuel loadings and fuel/stand relationships following a large-scale wind disturbance in the BWCAW helps describe not only the fuel loadings in the BWCAW and the surrounding forest ecosystem but also the ecosystem processes at work.

What We Found

Estimates of mean fuel loadings for the three study strata indicate that blowdown areas have nearly twice the 100- and 1,000-hr+ fuels as the non-blowdown BWCA area (Fig. 6). The means of 10-, 100-, and 1,000-hr+ fuel loadings in BWCAW blowdown areas were higher than those for these three classes in both the BWCAW non-blowdown areas and the Laurentian mixed-forest ecosystem of the Lake States (Bailey 1995) (Ecoregion 212; see Figure 32) (ANOVA, all $P < 0.1$, Fig. 6).

The size and decay classes of 1,000-hr+ fuels did not differ among the three study strata (Tables 2 and 3, ANOVA, $P > 0.4$). Fuels in the 3- to 8-inch diameter class accounted for 83 percent of the total number of 1,000-hr+ pieces/acre in BWCAW blowdown areas (Table 2). Similarly, the Ecoregion 212 and non-blowdown areas of the BWCAW had 84 and 86 percent of the total number of 1,000-hr+ pieces. The difference in the mean number of 1,000-hr+ fuels was not significant among the study strata for any decay class (Table 3).

Trees per acre and tons of down woody fuels per acre were not strongly related among the three study strata (Fig. 3). However, BWCAW blowdown locations had higher mean fuel loadings (Fig. 7) when trees per acre were low (0 to 303 tons/acre) compared to non-blowdown areas and Ecoregion 212. When the number of standing trees per acre was high, all three areas had similar mean total fuel loadings. Logically, one would expect blowdown areas to have fewer standing trees and more fuels. Areas less affected by blowdown would retain more standing trees, with fewer down trees, resulting in lower fuel levels. These expectations are supported by the blowdown observations in Figure 7.

Figure 6. Mean fuel class estimates for forested NRS FIA plots (ANOVA, all P < 0.1).

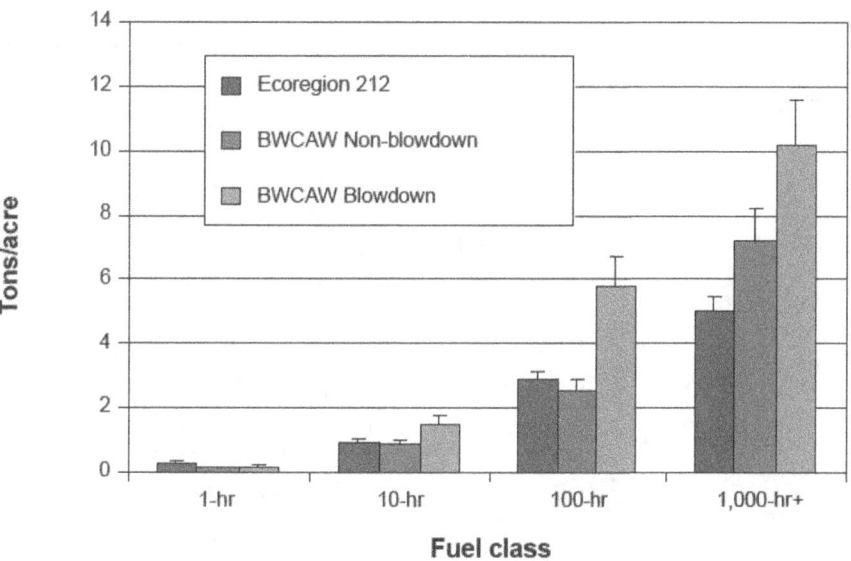

Figure 7. Mean total fuel estimates for three study areas (ANOVA, all P < 0.0001).

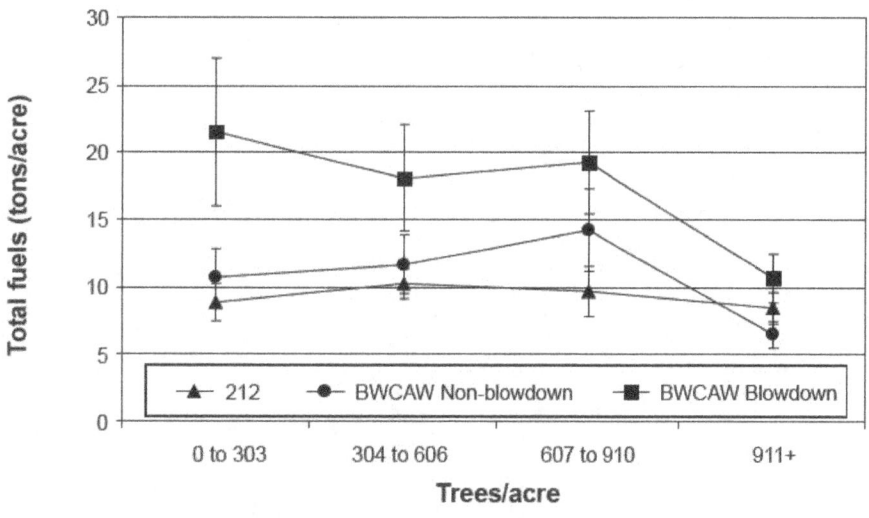

Table 2.—Mean 1,000-hr+ pieces/acre by diameter class and study area (ANOVA, P < 0.4)

Piece diameter (inches)	Pieces per acre (no.)								
	Ecoregion 212			BWCAW no damage			BWCAW damage		
	Mean	SE	Percent of total	Mean	SE	Percent of total	Mean	SE	Percent of total
3-8	155	9.7	84	159.5	20.2	86	167.1	21.4	83
8-13	25.9	2.4	14	25.1	3.6	14	31.6	4.5	16
13-18	2.4	0.4	1	0.8	0.4	0	2.4	0.8	1
19+	0.8	0.4	0	0	0	0	0.8	0.4	0

Table 3.—Mean 1,000-hr+ pieces/acre by decay class and study area (ANOVA, P > 0.3)

Decay class	Pieces per acre (no.)								
	Ecoregion 212			BWCAW no damage			BWCAW damage		
	Mean	SE	Percent of total	Mean	SE	Percent of total	Mean	SE	Percent of total
1	17	3	9	9	6	5	22	10	11
2	44	5	24	38	10	20	48	10	24
3	59	5	32	47	7	25	62	10	31
4	42	4	23	40	6	22	35	6	17
5	21	3	12	51	11	27	34	8	17

What This Means

Smaller diameter fuels decay quickly and disappear from wind-disturbed ecosystems, while larger fuels take longer to decay and thus remain in the ecosystem for longer periods. The greatest difference in fuel loadings among the study areas was for 100-hr fuels, which are the equivalent of large tree branches. The blowdown

dramatically increased fuel loadings of 100-hr fuels compared to other fuel classes. Therefore, large-scale blowdowns may have the greatest effect on limbs and crowns, detaching them from standing trees rather than knocking down the entire bole. There were significantly more 1,000-hr+ pieces in the BWCAW blowdown area, but the distribution of decay and size classes indicates that the accumulation of fuels from fallen trees is the same whether tree mortality was the result of normal processes, such as suppression mortality in Ecoregion 212, or large wind disturbances such as in the BWCAW blowdown.

In this study, we found no discernible relationship between total down woody fuel loadings and trees per acre. The amount of down woody fuel in Upper Great Lakes forests may be more dependent on successional trends and disturbance history (both natural and anthropogenic) than attributes for standing trees. Two stand development processes seem to confound correlations between these attributes and fuel loadings. First, some stands develop as a result of density-induced mortality and occasional individual-tree blowdowns (Canham and Loucks 1984, Frelich and Graumlich 1994). For these stands, a relatively constant amount of down woody materials can persist through all stages of stand development because of a balance between mortality and the decay of older woody materials. Other stands experience sudden stand-level disturbances, such as those observed in the blowdown areas of the BWCAW (see Canham and Loucks 1984, Frelich and Graumlich 1994, Peterson 2000, Woods 2004). For these stands, sudden reductions in stand density simultaneously increase fuel loadings. Both processes (small wind disturbances and infrequent, large wind catastrophes) appear to be occurring in Upper Great Lakes forests.

Effects of Blowdown on Overstory and Understory Diversity

Structural and species diversity is an important characteristic of most ecosystems, including the BWCAW. The pattern and intensity of disturbance influence both site-specific and landscape diversity. Identifying and understanding the storm's impact on diversity is an important research priority (Mattson and Shriner 2001).

What We Found

Even with a limited number of plots, we observed two interesting patterns. Where we had comparable forest types in blowdown and non-blowdown conditions, nearly every one showed a decline in overstory species diversity when we compared plots with no disturbance to those with weather damage (wind) (Table 4). Only aspen and other hardwoods and nonstocked forest-type groups showed a negligible change. When we examined understory diversity, measured by species richness, we found just the opposite: most of the blowdown sites showed increased diversity (Table 5). The exceptions were in paper birch and balsam fir forest types.

What This Means

Wind storms of similar magnitude to the storm in July 1999 can radically change the dynamics of a forest. Results suggest that some trees were damaged more heavily than others as large trees above the canopy may have been more susceptible to wind damage than trees just below the forest canopy. Such susceptibility would have reduced overstory diversity, as in the BWCAW. Yet this reduction increased opportunities for the understory vegetation community, probably due to the increased light level and reduced competition for soil moisture and nutrients. In the absence of further disturbances, overstory tree species again will dominate the site and return understory diversity to pre-1999 levels.

Table 4. Shannon index for overstory species diversity, by disturbance category and forest type (N = 53 plots).

Forest type	Disturbance category		Percent difference
	No disturbance	Weather	
All conifer forest types	1.12	1.03	-8
All hardwood forest types	1.25	1.01	-19
Aspen	1.29	1.28	0
Paper birch	1.34	1.00	-26
Sugar maple/beech/yellow birch	1.65		
Other hardwoods and nonstocked	0.86	0.85	0
Balsam fir	1.64	0.47	-71
Black spruce	0.95	0.78	-17
Eastern white pine	1.51		
Jack pine	0.89		
Northern white-cedar	0.89	1.05	18
White pine/red oak/white ash	2.09	1.75	-16
White spruce	1.36		
Other pine/hardwood	1.55		

Table 5. Understory species richness, by disturbance category and forest type (N = 53 plots).

Forest type	Disturbance category		Percent difference
	No disturbance	Weather	
All conifer forest types	19.6	21.0	7
All hardwood forest types	19.1	20.1	6
Aspen	19.3	20.0	3
Paper birch	22.2	19.4	-12
Sugar maple/beech/yellow birch	21.0		
Other hardwoods and nonstocked	12.3	25.0	103
Balsam fir	30.0	22.0	-27
Black spruce	19.3	25.5	32
Eastern white pine	19.5		
Jack pine	16.0		
Northern white-cedar	20.0	20.5	3
White pine/red oak/white ash	17.0	17.0	0
White spruce	16.0		
Other pine/hardwood	29.0		

THE RESOURCE AFTER THE BLOWDOWN

Forest Land Area

The chief motivation for setting aside the BWCAW was to preserve the land from further exploitation. Along with the tremendous water resources, the structure and diversity of the forests are the foundation of the Boundary Waters region. Of the BWCAW's 1.1 million acres, approximately 72 percent (783,000 acres) is forest land and 20 percent (190,000 acres) is open water. The forest land of the BWCAW is in a landscape diverse in geology, topography, disturbance history, and parcel size. Peninsulas, isthmuses, islands, lakes, ponds, rivers, and swamps create suitable conditions for numerous tree species in the North Woods. The forests of the Boundary Waters region vary by age, size, forest type, and forest-type group. NRS FIA defines a forest-type group as a collection of species grouped by co-occurrence, similar biological characteristics, or other factors.

What We Found

About 51 percent of forest land is covered by softwood types (Fig. 8) such as black spruce and jack pine. The remaining 49 percent is dominated by hardwood forest types. Seventeen forest-type groups were recorded during the 1999-2003 inventory: jack pine; red pine; eastern white pine; balsam fir; white spruce; black spruce; tamarack; northern white-cedar; white pine/red oak/white ash; other pine/hardwood; black ash/American elm/red maple; sugarberry/hackberry/elm/green ash; sugar maple/beech/yellow birch; elm/ash/locust; aspen; paper birch; and balsam poplar (Fig. 9). Seventy-one percent of total forest land area is represented by four forest types: paper birch (166,000 acres), aspen (164, 000 acres), black spruce (136,000 acres), and jack pine (92,000 acres). Sixty-two percent of total paper birch area (103,000 acres), 45 percent of total aspen area (74,000 acres), and 45 percent of total jack pine area (41,000 acres) was in medium-diameter trees (Fig. 9). Many of the forest-type groups, e.g., red pine and eastern white pine, had the bulk of the acreage in the medium- and large-diameter stand-size classes. Prominent exceptions were balsam fir, black spruce, tamarack, and black ash/American elm/red maple. Black spruce, which generally grows on sites that do not support rapid growth or large trees, has most of its acreage in the small and medium classes. This species generally averages 9 inches in diameter at maturity on good sites and 5 inches in diameter on poor sites. Tamarack can reach 20 inches in diameter on good sites but its average diameter is between 5 to 6 inches on nutrient-poor peatlands in northern Minnesota.

Figure 8. Forest land by forest type in the Boundary Waters Canoe Area Wilderness.

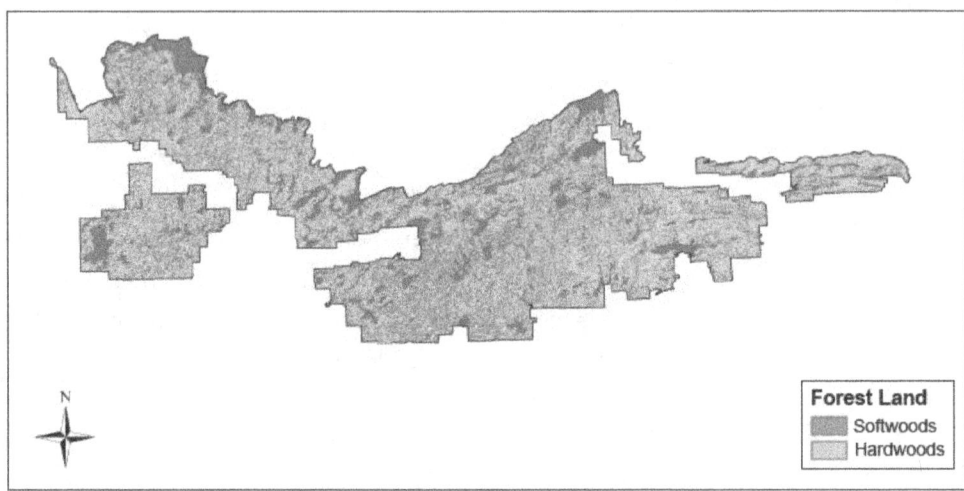

Figure 9. Area of forest land by forest type and stand-size class in the Boundary Waters Canoe Area Wilderness, 1999-2003.

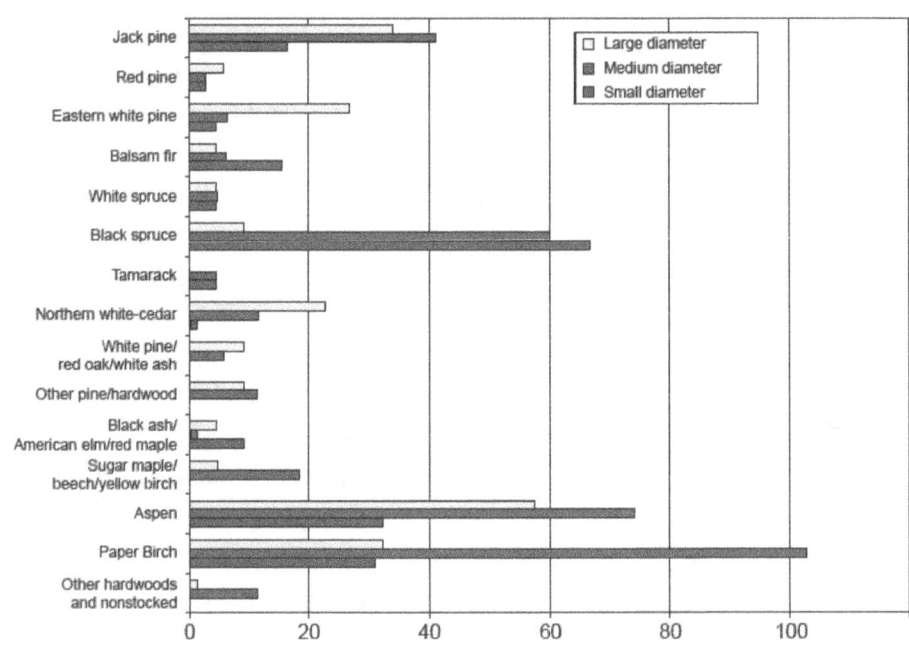

Forest land area (thousand acres)

What This Means

Tree diameter is not an accurate indicator of tree age in the BWCAW. Although small trees are sometimes associated with young stands in many forest types, the combination of low site quality and short growing seasons in the BWCAW confounds analyses of age vs. tree size. Although the BWCAW has high species and structural diversity, large disturbances still drive forest composition and structure. This conclusion is based on the dominance of four forest types—aspen, jack pine, paper birch, and black spruce—that rapidly colonize areas that are opened up by disturbances such as fire or windthrow. Nevertheless, disturbances are not consistent in their reach or impact; for example, a fire does not uniformly burn every acre. Therefore, the patchy nature of disturbance creates a variety of stands of different age and species composition.

Tree Number and Stand-size Class

An estimate of the number of trees in a forest can tell us something about its structure and often provides insight into the history of the stand. In general, productive sites with long growing seasons allow young trees to increase in diameter quickly. Therefore, a 9-inch tree with good crown position might be relatively young. However, in the BWCAW, where there is a short growing season and numerous low-productivity sites, a high number of medium-diameter stands does not always correlate with an abundance of middle-aged trees.

Stands generally start out with many small, young trees that become larger and less numerous as a result of competition-induced mortality. Therefore, a fully stocked stand with an average diameter less than 5 inches would have more trees per acre than a fully stocked stand where the average diameter exceeds 12 inches. Stand density is an important indicator of future stand dynamics because dense stands face higher competition for resources, e.g., light, water, and nutrients. Successful competition for resources helps determine species composition, growth rate, and general forest health. The combination of short growing seasons, low-productivity sites, and the presence of several species that tend to regenerate into dense stands of seedlings or sprouts and differentiate[1] slowly creates conditions for slow stand growth.

What We Found

There were an estimated 455 million live trees in the BWCAW in 1999-2003 (Fig. 10). The overall proportions were similar to those of the total forest area— 231 million trees (51 percent) were in the softwood species group versus 223 million trees in the hardwood-dominated forest types. There were more trees in medium-diameter stands for both softwood and hardwood types. Hardwoods had more trees than softwoods in medium-diameter stands, while softwoods had more trees in small-diameter stands (Fig. 10).

Most of the trees in the balsam fir and black spruce forest types were in small-diameter stands (Fig. 11 and Fig. 12a - Group A). Three of the four most prominent cover types (aspen, paper birch, and jack pine), had a preponderance of trees in the medium-diameter class (Fig. 11 and Fig. 12b - Group B). Finally, the red pine, eastern white pine (including white pine/red oak/white ash), white spruce, and northern white-cedar forest types had a plurality of trees in large-diameter stands (Fig. 11 and Fig. 12c - Group C).

---

[1]Differentiation is the process wherby groups of trees compete with each other, gain advantage, and grow (and die) at different rates. The ability of a tree species to respond to disturbance and gain advantage over its neighbors are two of the factors that determine whether that tree will become part of a future forest canopy.

What This Means

Each group of forest types represents a response to different disturbances. Group C consists of larger-diameter trees that likely are growing on a site that was previously disturbed. They probably are being replaced by younger and more shade-tolerant species. Group A is a mixture of two shade-tolerant forest types with different patterns of development. Black spruce can become established under closed canopies of shade intolerants but it also grows well in open sites. By contrast, balsam fir generally becomes established under canopies of pines, aspen, or birch. Black spruce is found on wet sites that limit growth and extend the time that trees remain small in diameter. The medium-size trees of Group B (aspen, birch, jack pine) might represent the passage of time since the last disturbance. A century of fire suppression means older trees have not been killed by wildfire and the growing conditions that facilitate regeneration of these species have not been created.

Figure 10. Number of all-live trees on forest land in the Boundary Waters Canoe Area Wilderness, 1999-2003.

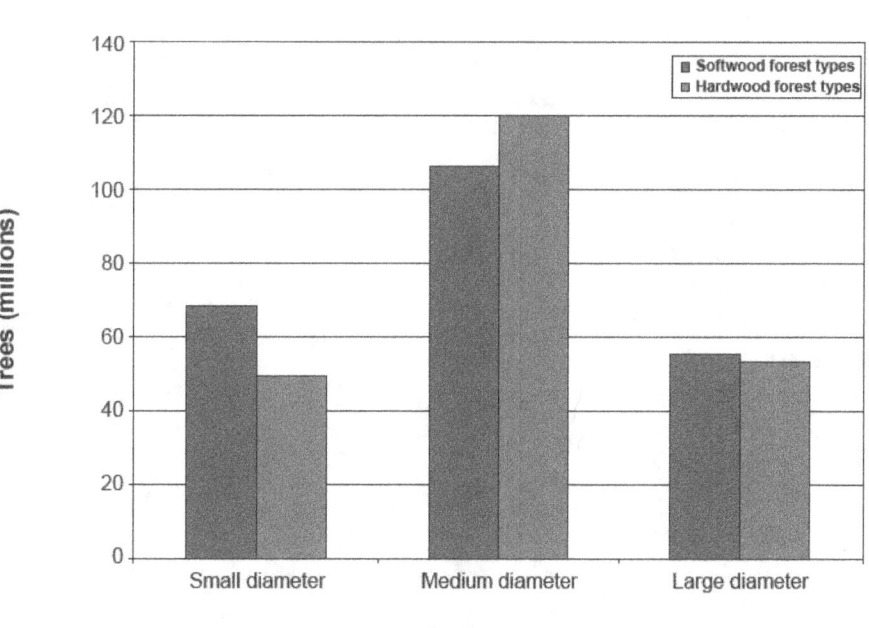

Figure 11. Number of trees in the Boundary Waters Canoe Area Wilderness, 1999-2003.

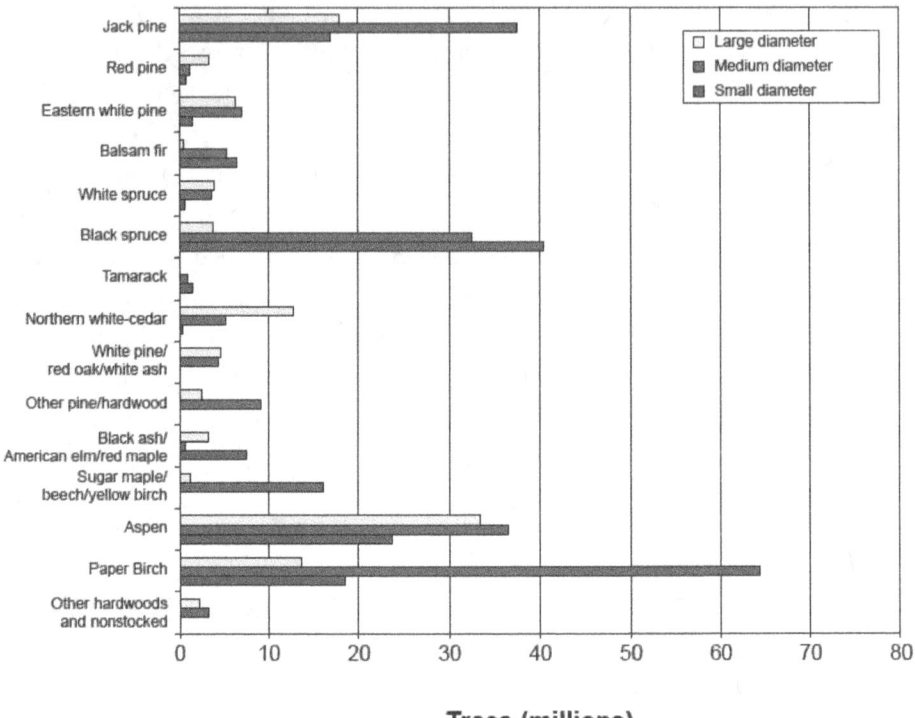

Trees (millions)

Figure 12. Patterns of diameter distribution vs. number of trees in the BWCAW: (a) plurality in stands with smaller trees, (b) plurality in stands with medium-size trees, (c) plurality in stands with larger trees (compare to the actual distribution of trees by forest type and diameter class in Figure 11).

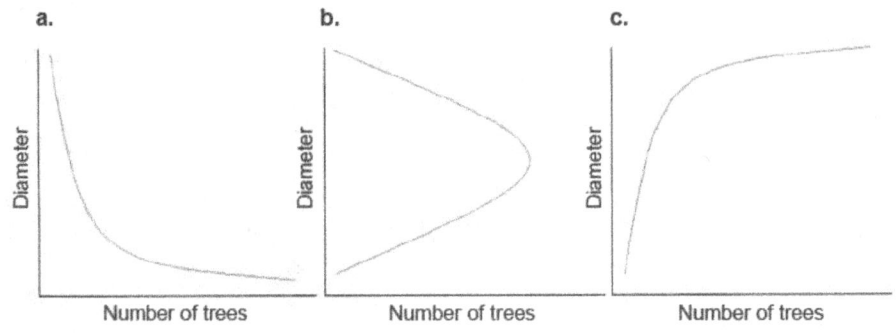

Volume

How much space does a tree occupy? The answer is determined using tree size; stem volume is a measure of tree size. The volume of all the trees in a forest is a function of the age of the species present, the productivity of the site, and growing conditions. Growing conditions include weather, disturbances, or other stressors. A forest with good site productivity, favorable growing conditions, and suitable species likely will have greater volume than it would on a poor site with a high level of disturbance and unsuitable species.

What We Found

In 1999-2003, all live-tree volume on forest land in the BWCAW was an estimated 832 million cubic feet (Fig. 13). Hardwoods accounted for 47 percent and softwoods accounted for 53 percent. Of this volume, 383 million cubic feet were in large-diameter stands, 400 million cubic feet were in medium-diameter stands, and 49 million cubic feet were in small-diameter stands. Seventy-two percent of total volume was in five forest types: jack pine (94 million cubic feet/11 percent), eastern white pine (84 million cubic feet/10 percent), black spruce (84 million cubic feet/10 percent), aspen (199 million cubic feet/24 percent), and paper birch (144 million cubic feet/17 percent) (Fig. 14).

Several forest types had most of their total volume in a particular stand-size class. Tamarack had all of its volume in medium- or small-diameter stands (Fig. 14). The volumes of elm/ash/locust and balsam poplar volume were mostly in medium-diameter stands. Ninety-four percent of red pine was in the large-diameter class and eastern white pine also had an overwhelming proportion of its total volume in large-diameter stands (Fig. 14). Both pines are capable of great size. White pine/red oak/ white ash and northern white-cedar both had more than 70 percent of their volume in large-diameter stands.

There are three stand-size classes: small-diameter trees (Fig. 15a - Class A), medium-size trees (Fig. 15b - Class B), and large-diameter trees (Fig. 15c - Class C). Most of the trees in jack pine stands were in medium-size stands, but there was more volume in large-diameter stands. Balsam fir and black spruce had more trees in small-diameter stands, though there was more volume in medium stands.

Seven species make up the bulk of total volume: quaking aspen, paper birch, northern white-cedar, eastern white pine, red pine, jack pine, and black spruce (Fig. 16). Monocultures are rare in the BWCAW. For example, quaking aspen is found in every major forest type; its proportion of total volume ranges from 4 percent of the sugar maple/beech/yellow birch type to nearly two-thirds of the aspen type. Paper birch also is found in many forest types. Most of the softwood species are commonly found in softwood forest types. Most of the hardwood types contain more species than softwood types.

What This Means

Two primary dynamics shape forest composition in the BWCAW: (1) pioneer species such as aspen or jack pine occupy gaps created by disturbances, and (2) late successional species like balsam fir start out in the understory. In the absence of disturbance, these species move into the overstory and eventually dominate the canopy. Shade-intolerant species establish in shade-tolerant forest types when a local disturbance creates gaps. While jack pine, paper birch, and aspen are opportunistic colonizers, continued lack of fire will progressively reduce the ecological opportunities for these species to establish and thrive.

Figure 13. Net volume of all-live trees in the Boundary Waters Canoe Area Wilderness, 1999-2003.

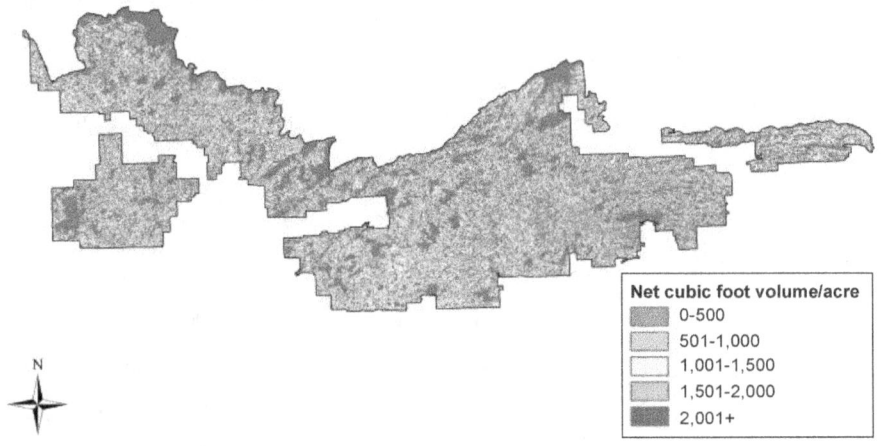

Net cubic foot volume/acre
- 0-500
- 501-1,000
- 1,001-1,500
- 1,501-2,000
- 2,001+

N

Figure 14. Volume of all-live trees on forest land in the Boundary Waters Canoe Area Wilderness, 1999–2003.

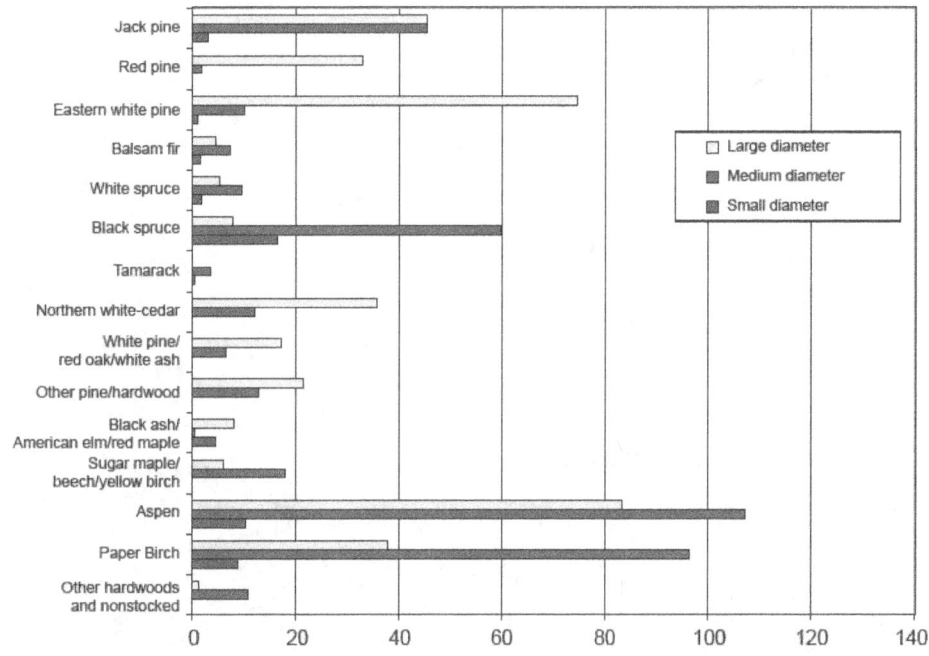

Volume of all live trees (million ft³)

Figure 15. Patterns of diameter distribution vs. all-live volume of trees in the Boundary Waters Canoe Area Wilderness: (a) plurality in stands with smaller trees, (b) plurality in stands with medium-size trees, (c) plurality in stands with larger trees (compare to the actual distribution of trees by forest type and diameter class in Figure 14).

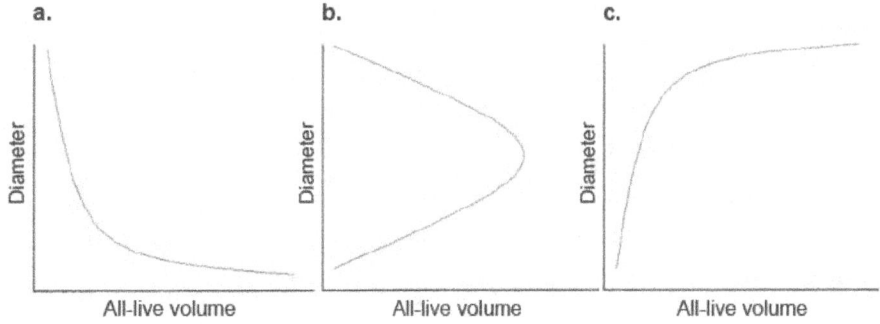

Figure 16. Volume of all-live trees, Boundary Waters Canoe Area Wilderness, 1999-2003.

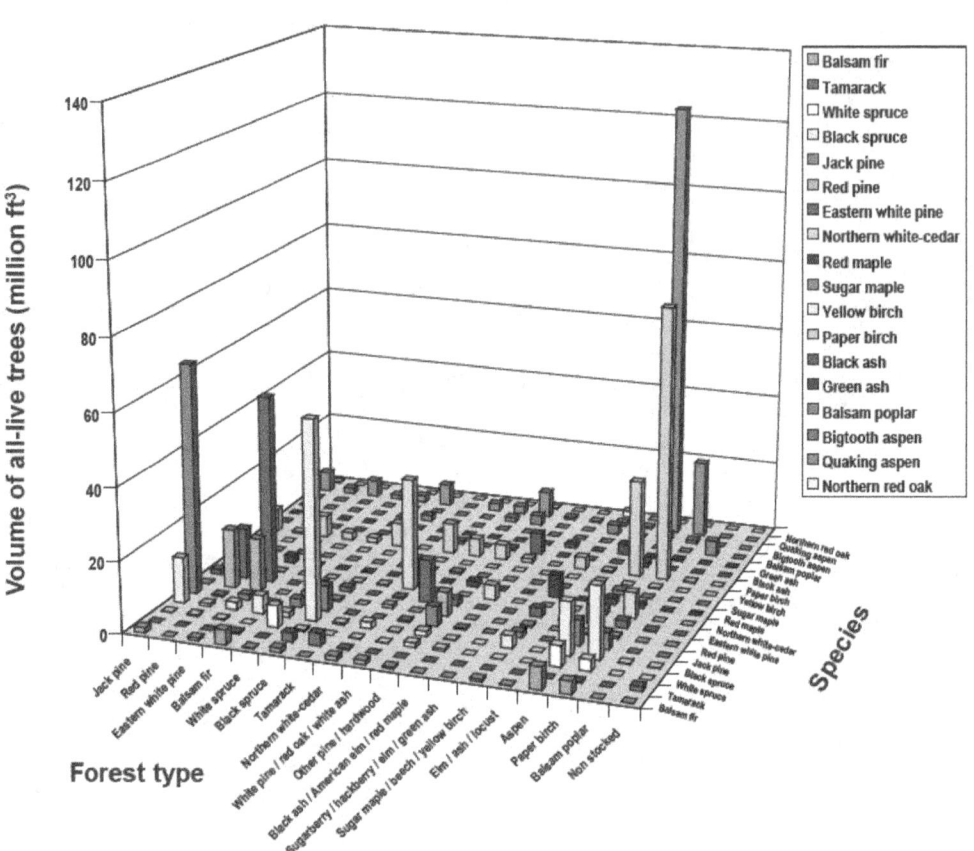

Species Composition and Diversity

Why tree-species diversity is important: forest health examples

A forest that includes a range of species, tree sizes, and ages can provide a variety of habitats for wildlife as well as a range of recreation and aesthetic experiences. Forest diversity influences and is influenced by forest health. For example, eastern spruce budworm, one of the most destructive insect defoliators in North America, defoliates millions of balsam fir and spruce trees annually. The budworm defoliates only new growth; feeding affects growth rates and trees will die after 7 years of defoliation. Since 1949, spruce budworm has defoliated balsam fir and white spruce in Minnesota every year but 1966. Black spruce is rarely defoliated and only when growing in association with balsam fir or white spruce. In the BWCAW, balsam fir and white spruce were defoliated 39 of the past 56 years. The most recent period of sustained defoliation occurred from 1983 to 1995; virtually all balsam fir and white spruce in the BWCAW were affected.

The forest tent caterpillar (FTC) has defoliated aspen 15 of the last 56 years. Repeated years of aspen defoliation can result in dieback and, in combination with drought, can cause tree mortality. Birch is occasionally defoliated by the FTC and is especially hard hit by drought and damage by the bronze birch borer and birch leaf miner. Old age also is a contributing factor. The most recent years of sustained defoliation occurred in 2000-2004.

Composition and structure of selected forest types

Jack pine, paper birch, and aspen. Three early successional forest types that rely on stand-replacing disturbances such as fire are jack pine, paper birch, and aspen (Fig. 17).

Figure 17. Location of selected forest types in the Boundary Waters Canoe Area Wilderness, 1999-2003.

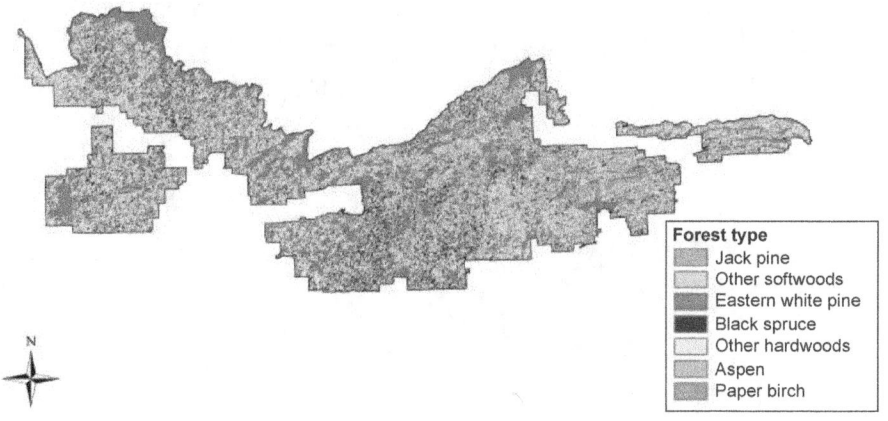

Forest type
- Jack pine
- Other softwoods
- Eastern white pine
- Black spruce
- Other hardwoods
- Aspen
- Paper birch

One of the most widespread conifers in northern North America, jack pine depends on fire to prepare sites for regeneration and to open its serotinous cones. Large jack pine trees are somewhat fire resistant but not as much as red pine or southern yellow pines. Paper birch, another early successional species, is a widespread hardwood tree that is valued by Native Americans. Pioneer species can be an indication of past disturbances, so they can help us determine stand history in the BWCAW. Quaking aspen is a widespread, aggressive colonizer of disturbed landscapes noted for its prolific sprouting and for its bright yellow leaves in the fall. Aspen represents a high proportion of total volume and total forest land area; its presence frequently points to the past occurrence of large disturbances. All three species can co-occur and frequently regenerate after the same disturbances (Heinselman 1973).

What We Found

Not surprisingly, the all-live volume in jack pine stands was dominated by jack pine trees (Fig. 18). However, it is interesting that aspen and paper birch, and black spruce, a more shade-tolerant and presumably late successional species, also had significant volume in the jack pine forest type. Black spruce becomes established after fires (Heinselman 1973) but also may have established under a jack pine overstory. In the absence of disturbance, black spruce may succeed jack pine as the dominant species in the overstory.

All-live volume in the paper birch forest type inside the BWCAW totaled 144 million cubic feet, of which 54 percent was paper birch (Fig. 19). Quaking aspen had 21.7 million cubic feet of volume in the paper birch type. Black spruce and northern white-cedar, two later successional species, had 20.3 and 7.3 million cubic feet of volume, respectively.

In the aspen forest type there were 182 million cubic feet of all-live volume. Sixty-eight percent or 124.1 million cubic feet resulted from the presence of quaking aspen (Fig. 20). The principal co-occurring species was paper birch (27.3 million cubic feet); jack pine volume was also high with 7.0 million cubic feet. There were 14.9 million cubic feet of black spruce volume and 6.2 million cubic feet of balsam fir volume in this forest type.

What This Means

Jack pine is an important early successional species in the BWCAW. The presence of this species as well as that of aspen and paper birch points to a stand-initiating disturbance, probably fire. All three forest types had significant volumes of later successional species, particularly in the smaller diameter classes. This characteristic hints at the presence or absence of fire. For example, having balsam fir as an understory companion to jack pine suggests that fire has not occurred since the stand was first regenerated. Balsam fir is one of few understory species that are likely to be much younger than the pioneer species in the overstory (Heinselman 1973). The data suggest that, in the absence of fire, these more shade-tolerant species will grow into the canopy and create the understory conditions that will favor only shade-tolerant advance regeneration.

Figure 18. All-live volume in the jack pine forest type, Boundary Waters Canoe Area Wilderness, 1999-2003.

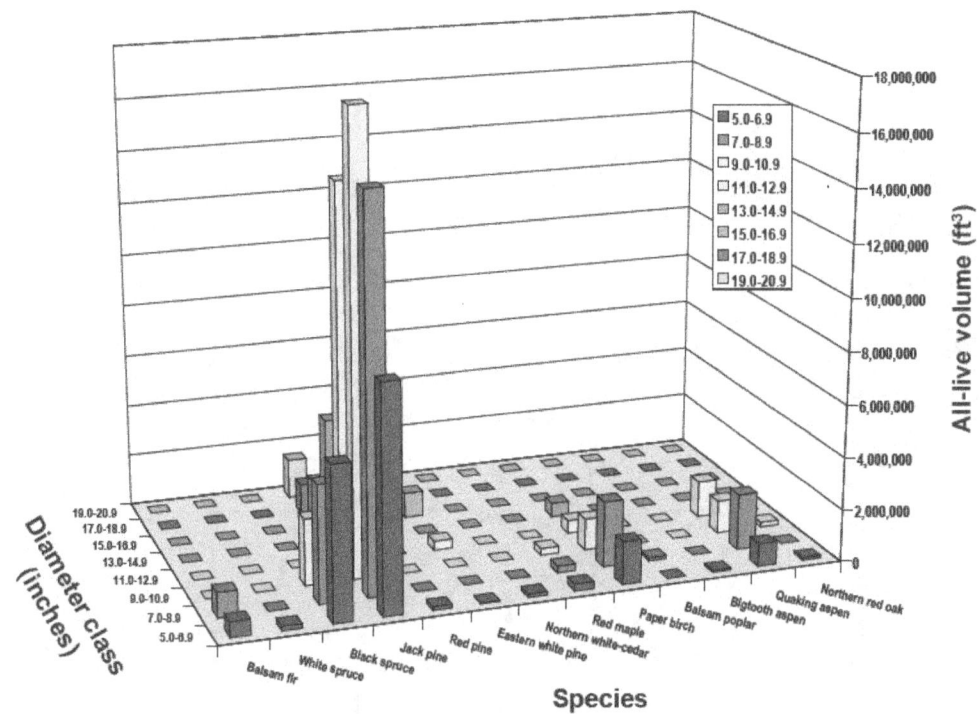

Figure 19. All-live volume in the paper birch forest type, Boundary Waters Canoe Area Wilderness, 1999-2003.

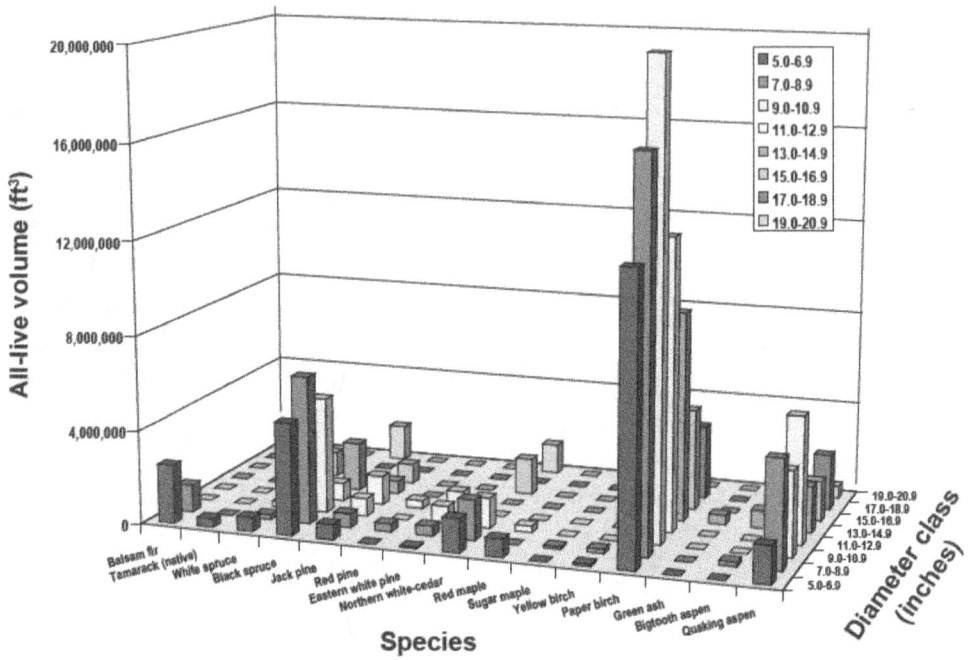

Figure 20. All-live volume in the aspen forest type, Boundary Waters Canoe Area Wilderness, 1999-2003.

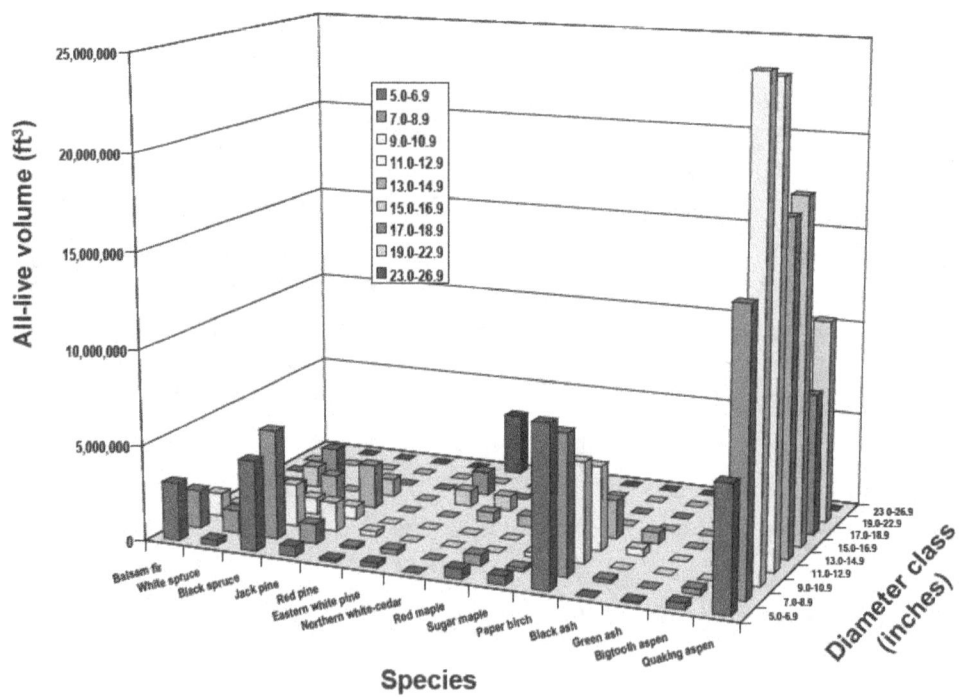

Eastern white pine. Majestic eastern white pines, emergent above the forested canopy, offer one of the most evocative images within the BWCAW. White pine forest land is abundant in area (Fig. 9) and volume (Fig. 14). Eastern white pine and red pine once covered about 20 percent of the area in the BWCAW (Ayres 1899). Because white pine is somewhat resistant to fire, its presence can be tied to periods of disturbance. Due to logging and uncontrolled fires (natural and human caused), it occupies much less area today.

What We Found

Most eastern white pine stands are 61 to 100 years old (Fig. 21). Most of the remaining volume falls into the 21 to 40 and 161 to 180 age groups. The large presence of paper birch and aspen in the 61 to 100 year age group suggests that the forest type was established by a significant disturbance not repeated in subsequent years.

Figure 21. All-live volume in the eastern white pine forest type, Boundary Waters Canoe Area Wilderness, 1999-2003.

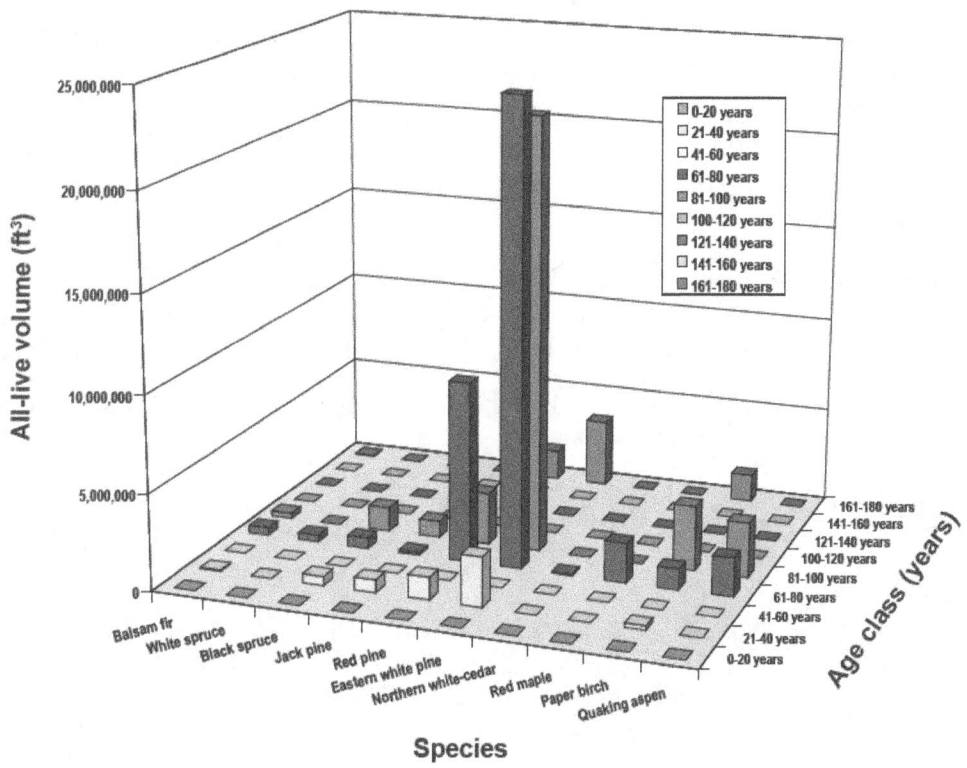

What This Means

Diversity resulting from the interaction between factors such as site, species, and disturbance history is a recurring theme in nearly every acre of forest land in the BWCAW. One example concerns eastern white pine. Because the bulk of the white pine volume was in the 61 to 100 year age class and mature white pine is moderately fire resistant, it is likely that disturbances between 1899 to 1942 created conditions suited to white pine and its cohorts. The presence of red pine, birches, and aspen in similar age classes also suggest a fire origin of the stand. Because of the relative fire resistance of mature pines with thick bark, fire does not necessarily result in the initiation of a new stand (Heinselman 1973). A fire might not kill the overstory (releasing growing space) but would kill seedlings in the understory. The reason for the lack of young stands might be that the overstory density reached a point where any seedling that did germinate was unable to survive under the canopy.

What We Found

Late successional forest type: sugar maple/birch/beech. A variation of the maple/birch/beech forest type is common in the eastern portion of the BWCAW, where red maple (*A. rubrum*) is the largest component. The forest type has a fairly varied composition (Fig. 22). In addition to red maple there were significant volumes of paper birch, bigtooth aspen, eastern white pine, black spruce, and jack pine. The oldest age class for all four forest types was 61 to 80 years. Judging from the fact that thin-barked red maple was able to establish, these data suggest that fire was limited from 1920 to 1960. This gap fits neatly into Heinselman's (1973) period of fire suppression in the North Woods.

What This Means

As we have observed with other forest types, there apparently was a gap in the normal disturbance regime, allowing the maple/birch/beech forest type to become established. The range of age classes in this type is striking in its limited extent, particularly when considering the range of potential maximum ages of the BWCAW's forests.

Figure 22. All-live volume in the sugar maple/yellow birch/beech forest type, Boundary Waters Canoe Area Wilderness, 1999-2003.

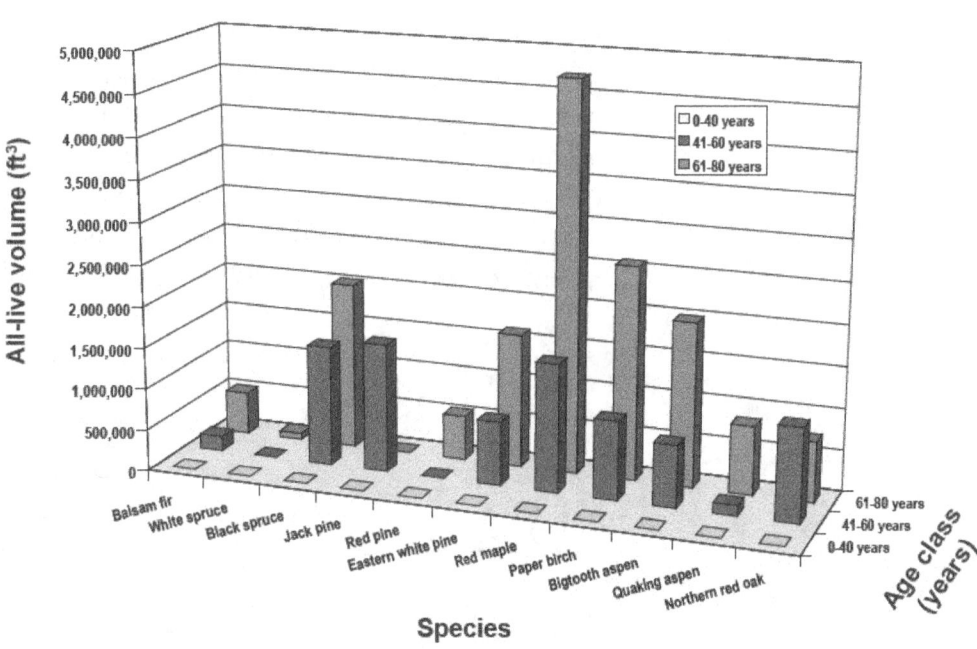

Diversity of overstory species

One measure of diversity is the number of species in a plot, stand, or region. This "species richness" treats species' presence equally, whether there are 2 trees or 2,000. By contrast, the Shannon diversity index measures a combination of the number of species and the evenness or distribution of those species (Magurran 2003). A forest with 10 species where 90 percent of the area is occupied by a single species will have a lower Shannon index than a forest with 10 species where each of the species occupies a roughly equal proportion of the forest area. As in our example, the absolute magnitude of the index is not important; its value is as a relative index for comparing different landscapes (Peet 1975).

What We Found

There are pockets of high and low tree species diversity in BWCAW forests. When estimates of the overstory Shannon diversity index were compared to overstory basal area (Table 6), the diversity index appeared to stabilize after the basal area reached a certain threshold. For example, jack pine diversity appeared to stabilize around 1.2 after a basal area of 30 square feet per acre. There were no trends for diversity vs. age (Table 7). Aspen and paper birch diversity appear to be consistent across age classes unlike jack pine diversity, which increased as age increased and black spruce diversity, which declined with age.

What This Means

Although site or climatic factors can limit the number of species on a particular site, diversity often is influenced by each tree species' competitive abilities, the collective associations of tree species, and site productivity or human interactions that attempt to direct a forest toward a particular structure or species mix. Given that the overstory diversity of each forest type is stable by basal area but varies by age, except for aspen and paper birch, we can conclude that time since the last major disturbance is the primary driver of diversity in the BWCAW.

Table 6. Average Shannon diversity index of overstory tree species, by forest type and overstory basal area, Boundary Waters Canoe Area Wilderness, 1999-2003.

Forest type	Overstory basal area (ft²/acre)													
	10	20	30	40	50	60	70	80	90	100	110	120	130	160
Aspen	--	--	--	1.3	--	1.7	1.3	1.1	1.5	--	1.2	--	1.5	--
Black spruce	--	--	1.6	0.9	0.7	--	0.7	1.0	0.7	1.0	--	--	--	--
Eastern white pine	--	--	--	--	--	--	--	1.5	--	--	--	--	--	1.5
Jack pine	0.3	--	--	--	--	1.3	--	--	--	--	--	--	0.7	--
Paper birch	--	0.5	1.2	1.2	1.2	0.9	0.8	1.4	1.2	--	--	1.1	--	--
White pine/red oak/ white ash	--	--	--	--	1.7	2.1	--	--	--	--	--	--	--	--

Table 7. Average Shannon diversity index of overstory tree species, by forest type and average stand age class, Boundary Waters Canoe Area Wilderness, 1999-2003.

Forest type	Average stand age (years)										
	0	10	30	40	50	60	70	80	90	100	110
Aspen	--	1.32		1.43	0.69	1.21	1.22	1.53	1.28	--	--
Balsam fir	--	--	--	1.64	--	--	--	--	--	0.47	--
Black spruce	--	--	--	1.15	0.95	1.32	0.33	--	0.16	--	0.86
Eastern white pine	--	--	--	--	--	--	--	1.53	1.49	--	--
Jack pine	--	0.35	--	0.61	--	--	--	--	2.00	--	--
Paper birch	0.89	--	--	--	1.23	1.18	1.19	1.05	--	--	--

Species composition and diversity of understory vegetation

Understory species composition. Understory vegetation is an important component of forested ecosystems. Changes in the diversity and abundance of vascular plant species can indicate stress, e.g., pollution or forest degradation. Another indicator of disturbance is an increase in the number of exotic species, many of which are early colonizers (pioneer) species.

What We Found

Of the 214 species in understory vegetation plots, 167 were in hardwood forest types and 165 in softwood forest types. Forty-seven were only in softwood types while 49 were only in hardwood types. In softwood forest types (Fig. 23), 4 of the top 15 understory vegetation species (5 in hardwood types (Fig. 24)) were regenerating trees, that is, young seedlings that will grow into the canopy should growing space become available. There were six species of woody shrubs in softwood types and four in hardwood forest types. Of the remaining understory vegetation species, four were herbaceous species, including large-leaved aster, *Eurybia macrophylla*, and one was a forb, *Aralia nudicaulis* or wild sarsaparilla. Although they varied in importance, whether in hardwood or softwood forest types, the 15 most common species were largely the same. The only difference was the presence of quaking aspen (*Populus tremuloides*) in hardwood forests and late low blueberry (*Vaccinium angustifolium*) in softwood forest types.

What This Means

The BWCAW landscape is dominated by four fire-influenced forest types: jack pine, quaking aspen, paper birch, and black spruce. Given the importance of past fires in regenerating these forest types and a history of fire suppression, it is not surprising to find nearly identical species in the softwood and hardwood types. In such early successional forest types, the time since the stand-initiating disturbance, soils, and climate have the most significant influence on species composition.

Figure 23. Top 15 understory species in softwood forest types based on the number of plots with at least one instance of the species, Boundary Waters Canoe Area Wilderness, 1999-2003.

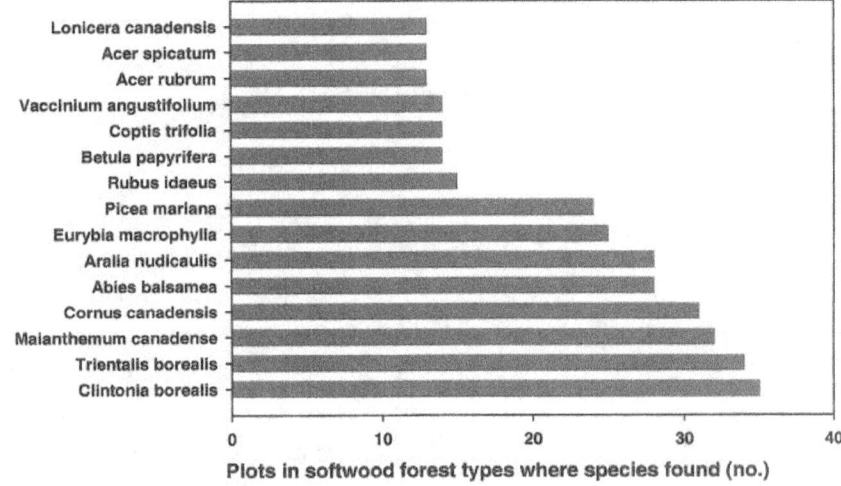

Figure 24. Top 15 understory species in hardwood forest types based on the number of plots with at least one instance of the species, Boundary Waters Canoe Area Wilderness, 1999-2003.

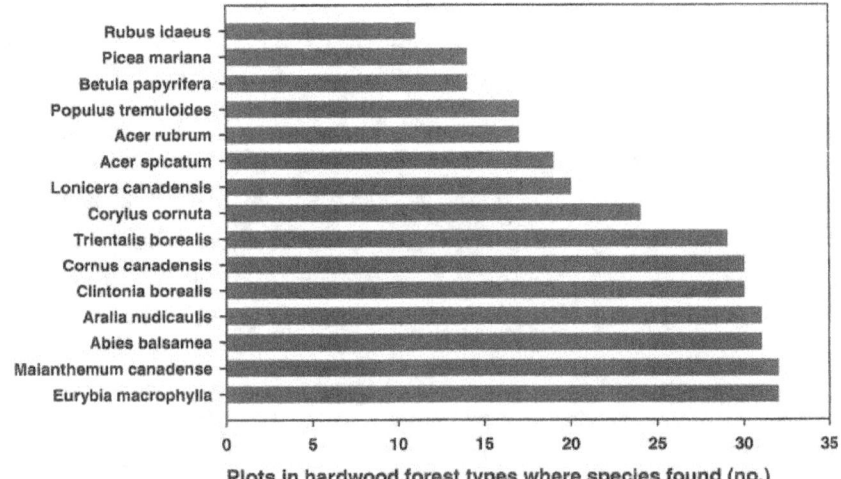

Understory species diversity. The overstory influences the presence, vigor, and composition of tree and other plant species in the understory. An open canopy allows maximum sunlight to reach the forest floor as well as minimum overstory competition for soil moisture, which favors certain plant species. This type of overstory provides less protection from the elements than a dense canopy, which shuts out more light and provides increased root competition, which again favors certain species. Depending on forest type, there might be an increase or decrease in diversity as the overstory basal area increases.

What We Found

We compared the number of species with forest type and overstory basal-area class. Shade-intolerant pioneer species allow more light through their canopies. A completely open canopy might resemble open grassland, with the majority of biomass in a relatively limited suite of species. Understory diversity was higher at lower basal areas of shade-tolerant forest types and at higher basal areas for shade-intolerant forest types, e.g., aspen and birch (Table 8).

What This Means

Although a limited number of samples precludes firm conclusions about species and forest types, we found interesting trends. First, early successional forests have more species in the understory than late successional forests with the same overstory basal area, because the early successional canopy lets in more light. In some inconclusive instances, forest types such as aspen had slightly higher species richness. Another implication is that the number of understory species varied little over most of the forest types and basal areas. This suggests that overall regional productivity and climate, as well as the disturbance regime, influenced understory diversity more than the forest type in the overstory.

Table 8. Understory species richness, by forest type and basal area, Boundary Waters Canoe Area Wilderness, 1999-2003

Forest type	Basal area (ft²/acre)													
	10	20	30	40	50	60	70	80	90	100	110	120	130	160
Aspen	--	--	--	9	--	20	20	20.5	16	--	25	--	22	--
Black spruce	--	--	16	28	18	--	23	16	15.5	25	--	--	--	--
Eastern white pine	--	--	--	--	--	--	--	17	--	--	--	--	--	22
Jack pine	15	--	--	--	--	18.5	--	--	--	--	--	--	12	--
Paper birch	--	18	17	22	20	18	20	23	21	--	--	19	--	--
White pine/red oak/white ash	--	--	--	--	17	17	--	--	--	--	--	--	--	--

Invasive species. The spread of nonnative invasive plants threatens species diversity and productivity throughout North America and the world. Intentionally or not, hundreds of nonnative species have been introduced to the United States. One of the most important benefits of protected areas like BWCAW is that humans have a minimum impact on native plant communities.

What We Found

Six species of nonnative invasive understory plants were found on NRS FIA plots in the BWCAW and more than half were grasses. Included were *Poa trivialis* (six occurrences), *Poa pratensis* and *Sonchus oleraceus* (two each) and *Humulus lupulus*, *Lychnis coronaria*, and *Rosa rugosa* (one each). Despite many homesteads and in-holdings in the BWCAW, there does not seem to be a great number of invasive species. However, officials with the SNF found evidence of other invasive species, including orange and yellow hawkweeds (*Hieracium aurantiacum* and *H. caespitosum*) and spotted knapweed (*Centaurea maculosa*) (Bruce Anderson, SNF, pers. comm.).

What This Means

Invasive species can alter ecosystem processes and structure. Although we did not find numerous invasive plant species in the BWCAW, more time must be devoted to identifying such species as the number of people visiting the region increases, thus increasing the transport and spread of nonnative invasive species.

Age

The age of a forest tells a story about the land's productivity, its disturbance history, and the events and interactions among its constituent parts. Age can influence rate of growth, suitability for a particular species of wildlife, or potential for economic use, and also alter susceptibility and response to disturbance. Expectations about the relationships between age and species composition, age and size, and age and growth rate are based on ecological knowledge. The age structure of the BWCAW reflects the impact of at least two factors: exclusion from harvesting of certain areas and influence of past disturbances such as wind storms, insects and disease attacks, and fire regimes.

Age is a difficult variable to interpret using NRS FIA data. The age of a stand is estimated from tree cores of two or three dominant or codominant trees in the overstory and may not represent the age of the stand as a whole. It is tempting to use tree size as a surrogate for tree age, particularly when not all trees are sampled. The NRS FIA stand-size variable provides a coarse surrogate for stages of stand development (McWilliams et al. 2002), but it is based solely on tree diameter, which, in turn, can be influenced by tree density, site conditions, disturbance history and species, and other factors. For example, a fast-growing 40-year-old aspen stand might have a greater average diameter than an 80-year-old black spruce stand. For these reasons, care is needed when looking at size alone.

What We Found

The youngest stands apparently predominate in the east-central and western portions of the BWCAW, while the older stands are more prominent in the central and northwestern portions (Fig. 25). Looking at total forest land area, some of the forest-type groups like jack pine have significant amounts of acreage in each age class, reflecting more frequent stand-initiating past disturbances (Fig. 26). Other types seem to have been initiated at one time.

Black spruce had the most even distribution of volume among age classes (Fig. 27). Except for the 0- to 20-year age class, which would have been expected to have little biomass, the proportion of volume roughly matches the proportion by area (Fig. 26). Red pine had a much higher proportion of its volume in older stands (81+ years). The two most prominent species, quaking aspen and paper birch, had most of their biomass in the 40- to 80-year age classes (Fig. 27). Of interest is how many forest types have most of their total volume in these classes, particularly among hardwood forest types. Of the 17 forest types in the BWCAW, 10 have at least 60 percent of their volume in these age classes.

What This Means

Ecological preservation, wildlife habitat, and wilderness recreation are not the only benefits provided by the BWCAW. Another benefit comes from the opportunity for carbon sequestration, an ecological function whereby growing vegetation captures and stores carbon, resulting in reduced levels of atmospheric carbon, which is a greenhouse gas. As we look to forests in the North Woods as reservoirs of carbon storage, we need to understand age-class and species mix, both of which strongly influence carbon accumulation, to understand the disturbance history that created these age- and species-mixes.

Heinselman (1973) defined the natural fire rotation as the average time required for a natural fire regime to burn an area equivalent to the total area of an ecosystem. This concept is valuable in comparing disturbance patterns in different ecosystems and attempting to understand the degree to which many plant species depend on fire. Heinselman estimated a presettlement fire rotation of 122 years, settlement fire rotation of 87 years, and a fire-rotation value of 2,000 years for the 61-year span of fire suppression between 1911 and 1972—a dramatic change. This period of fire suppression is evident in the high proportion of 40- to 80-year-old volume in the BWCAW. On the basis of these data alone, we conclude that: (1) stand-replacing disturbances have not occurred for some time, and (2) if such disturbances do not occur in the future, there will be a change in forest type as the shade intolerants reach the canopy and outlive the early successional aspen and birch.

Figure 25. Stand age in the Boundary Waters Canoe Area Wilderness, 1999-2003.

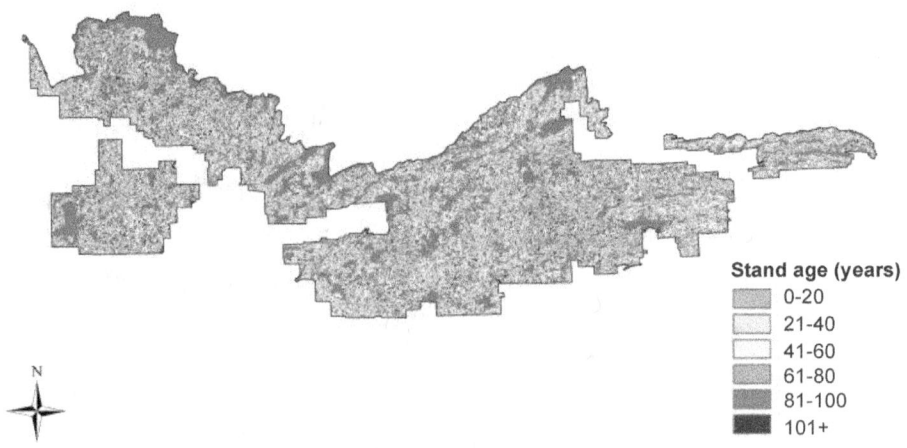

Stand age (years)
- 0-20
- 21-40
- 41-60
- 61-80
- 81-100
- 101+

Figure 26. Total forest-land area of the Boundary Waters Canoe Area Wilderness, 1999-2003.

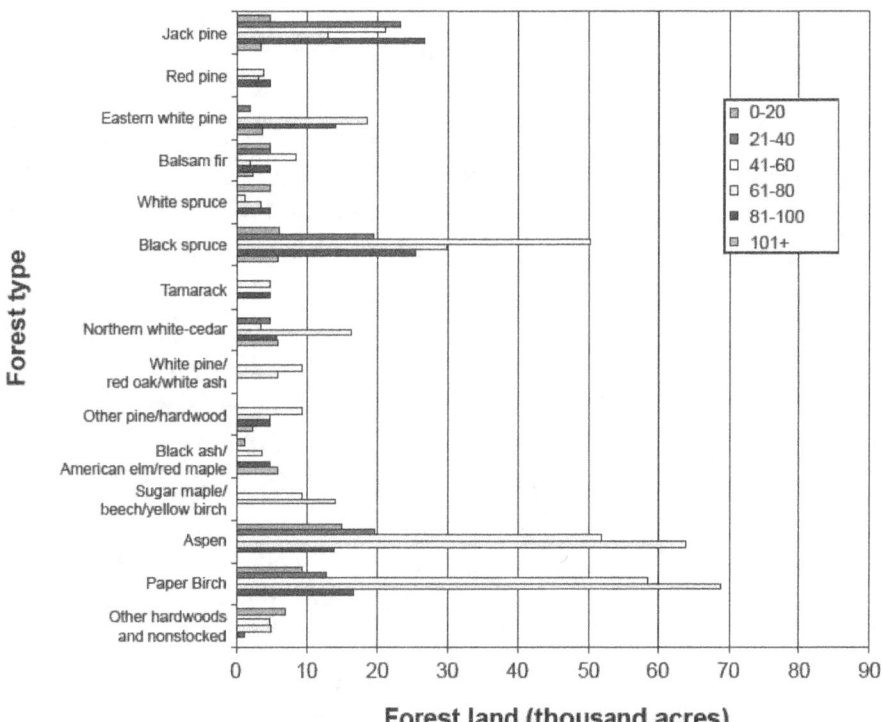

Figure 27. All-live volume in the Boundary Waters Canoe Area Wilderness, 1999-2003.

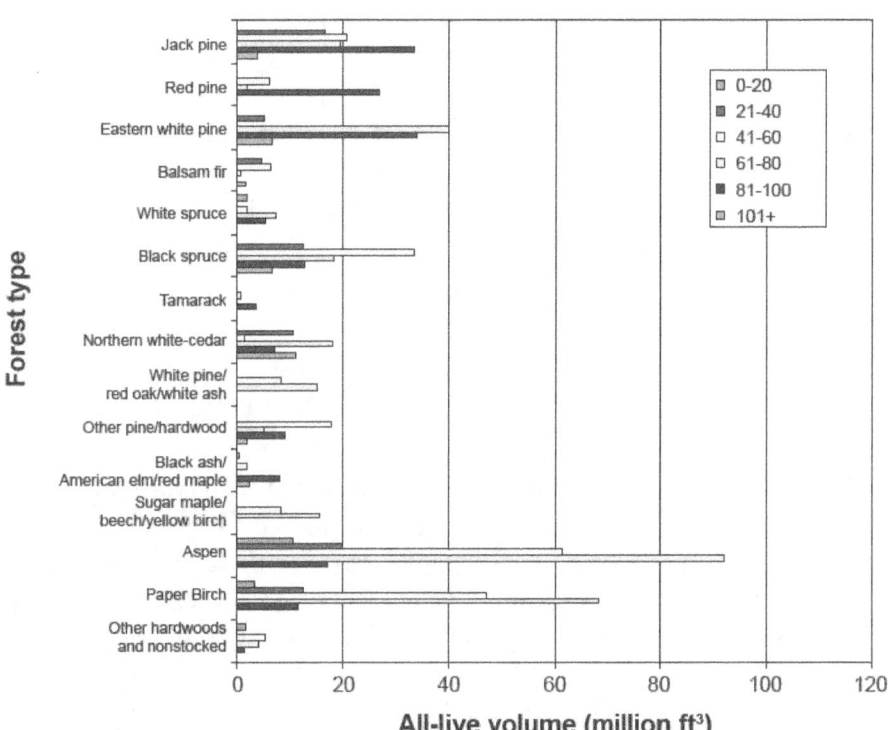

Soil Resource of the BWCAW

Climate and soils have a profound influence on the forests of the BWCAW. Inventory and assessment of the forest soils provide critical baseline information on forest health and productivity, especially in light of continued natural and human disturbance. The forests of the BWCAW are underlain largely by inceptisols, entisols, and histosols (Fig. 28). Inceptisols are diverse and relatively young soils that have not experienced extreme weathering or major accumulation of metal oxides. They occur across a range of climates and vegetative communities. Entisols are mineral soils that might only have the beginnings of a soil horizon. In Minnesota, they are common in river bottoms and outwash sands. Histosols generally have a high organic matter content in the upper 30 inches; these are the marsh and bog soils found in ancient glacial lake beds across the northern part of the State (Anderson et al. 2001, Brady 1990, Spurr and Barnes 1980, USDA Natural Resource Conservation Service 1999). The peaty or "hemist" type of histosols are common in northern Minnesota, where the cool climate slows decomposition. The nature of histosols makes it difficult to obtain consistently accurate volume measurements in the field. Accordingly, density and chemistry data from this soil type are limited.

Soils data were collected from 2001-2003 (Table 9). Because data were limited, it was difficult to compare soils under different forest-type groups. Therefore, we considered only a few forest-type groups with more than five samples. Coniferous forest-type groups were found on deeper soils than the aspen/birch forest-type group (Fig. 29). The forest floors[2] under softwood forest-type groups in Minnesota are thicker than those under hardwood forest-type groups (Miles et al. 2007), but the small number of samples limits our ability to draw a similar conclusion in the BWCAW. The relative carbon content of the forest floor is consistent across forest-type groups (Fig. 30). The white/red/jack pine forest-type group has lower soil pH (0-4 in) than the aspen/birch forest-type group (Fig. 31). The calcium:aluminum ratio is lowest in the white/red/jack pine forest-type group (Table 9), suggesting that these forest-type groups are underlain by poor quality soils. Under certain conditions, aluminum can be toxic to plants.

Softwood forests tend to accumulate greater amounts of forest floor than hardwood stands because of the chemical properties of the litter itself. Softwood needles tend to have lower nutrient content and thus break down more slowly than hardwood leaves. The difference also may be related to outbreaks of exotic earthworms that consume hardwood litter. These outbreaks are known to adversely affect rare plants, nutrient cycling, and the broader plant community (Bohlen et al. 2004a, b; Gundale 2002; Hale et al. 2005; Pritchett and Fisher 1987).

---

[2]FIA defines the forest floor as the entire thickness of organic material overlying the mineral soil, consisting of the litter and the duff (humus) (O'Neill et al., 2005).

The low soil pH, high aluminum, and low ECEC are related to the chemistry of the coniferous litter. Coniferous litter is more acidic than deciduous litter (Pritchett and Fisher 1987), so low pH leachate percolates through the soil profile. The hydrogen ions tend to displace the native minerals useful for plant growth and lower the pH of the mineral soil (Brady 1990). Aluminum is increasingly mobilized as soil pH decreases (McBride 1994). These are natural processes that can lead to the formation of spodosols.

Figure 28. Soil orders in Minnesota. In northeastern Minnesota, forests are concentrated on alfisols and inceptisols. Entisols and histosols also are prominent forest soils.

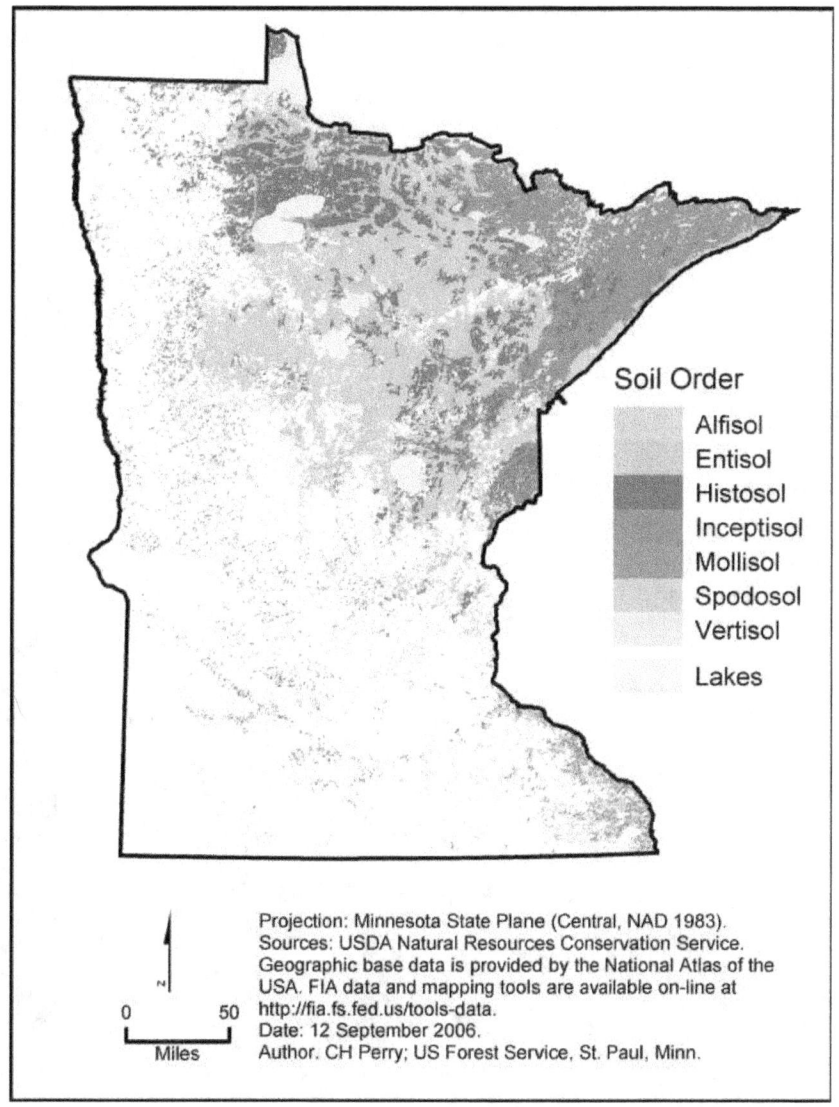

Soil Order

Alfisol
Entisol
Histosol
Inceptisol
Mollisol
Spodosol
Vertisol

Lakes

0   50

Miles

Projection: Minnesota State Plane (Central, NAD 1983).
Sources: USDA Natural Resources Conservation Service.
Geographic base data is provided by the National Atlas of the USA. FIA data and mapping tools are available on-line at http://fia.fs.fed.us/tools-data.
Date: 12 September 2006.
Author. CH Perry; US Forest Service, St. Paul, Minn.

Table 9. Selected chemical
properties of the mineral soil,
Boundary Waters Canoe Area
Wilderness, 2001-2003.

Layer and forest type group	No. samples	pH	Org. C (%)	Ex. Ca (mg/kg)	Ex. Al (mg/kg)	ECEC (cmol+/kg)
Forest floor						
White/red/jack pine	14		39.82			
Spruce/fir	10		34.99			
Aspen/birch	21		39.47			
Mineral soil (0-10 cm)						
White/red/jack pine	6	4.23[a]	6.91	482.62[a]	399.34[a]	7.96
Spruce/fir	6	4.65[ab]	3.65	551.79[ab]	241.53[ab]	6.16
Aspen/birch	12	4.70[b]	4.03	900.95[b]	131.74[b]	8.19
Mineral soil (10-20 cm)						
White/red/jack pine	4	5.06	3.55	387.07	91.77	3.80
Spruce/fir	5	5.12	2.22	587.97	126.22	5.16
Aspen/birch	9	4.90	2.09	292.77	160.83	3.83

Superscripts are used to indicate which means are statistically similar. All observations are statistically
similar in those groups without any superscripts.

Figure 29. Depth to subsoil,
Boundary Waters Canoe Area
Wildnerness, 2001-2003. Error
bars represent 1 standard
error.

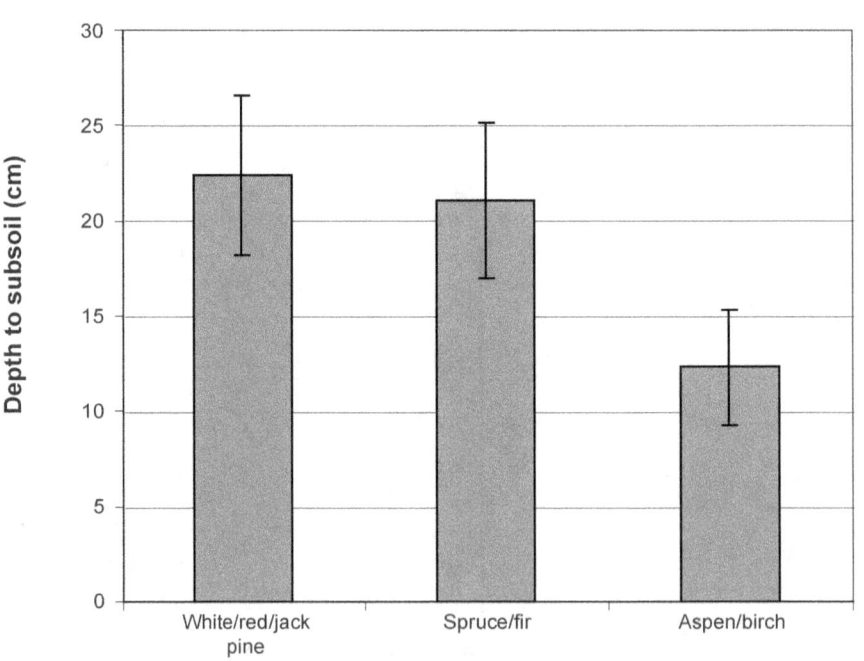

Figure 30. Organic carbon in the forest floor, Boundary Waters Canoe Area Wilderness, 2001-2003. Error bars represent 1 standard error.

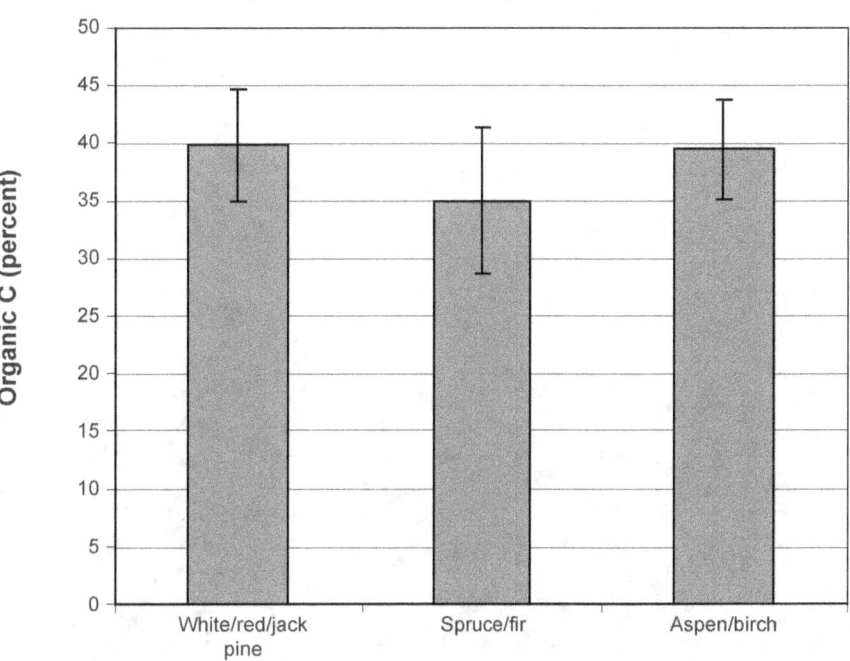

Figure 31. pH of the mineral soil (0 to 4 inches), Boundary Waters Canoe Area Wilderness, 2001-2003. Error bars represent 1 standard error.

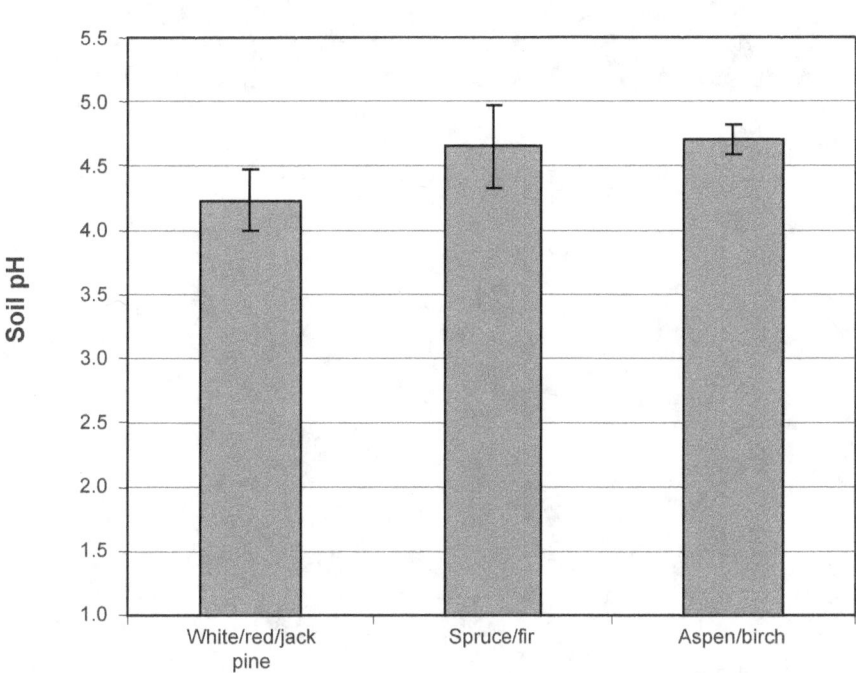

Heinselman (1973) emphasized that a variety of disturbances, interacting with variation in landscapes and species, has resulted in incredible diversity in the BWCAW. Formed by a complex interplay of disturbance, land, and climate, the forests of the BWCAW contain a variety of stand structures, species mixes, and densities that provide us with a myriad of wilderness experiences.

Diversity, particularly structural diversity, is threatened by the suppression of these disturbances. Efforts have been made to reestablish fire as a tool for shaping stand structure and composition, but the large-scale, irregular wildfires that played such a prominent role in shaping the current state of the forests are unlikely to occur again.

Wind damage, at both small and large scales, can radically alter the forest. We have seen how the dramatic changes caused by the 1999 windstorm have affected the BWCAW's forests with respect to volume, composition, structure, and diversity. The dramatic increase in down woody material increases the risk of catastrophic fire, particularly in the short term, until such fuels are reduced.

As we continue into the 21st century, areas like the BWCAW not only have ecological value but also offer recreational and spiritual refuges from the rapid pace of modern life. The BWCAW, while changing at a pace far different from that of landscapes outside its boundaries, continues to change. In fact, the BWCAW of the 22nd century may be far different from what we see today depending on the frequency of disturbances that nature and humans cause.

Inventory Plots

The plot and tree measurements presented here are from measurements on 211 forest inventory plots between September 1998 and August 2003 as part of the national inventory conducted by the USDA Forest Service's Forest Inventory and Analysis (FIA) program (Table 10) (Bechtold and Patterson 2005). These permanent sample plots are located systematically at an intensity of approximately one plot every 3,000 acres. The data used in this study were restricted to plots in the Boundary Waters Canoe Area Wilderness, Superior National Forest, Minnesota, and further restricted to plots that were entirely on forest land. Complete documentation of the plot design and all measurements can be found at http://socrates.lv-hrc.nevada.edu/fia/dab/databandindex.html.

Tree measurements used include species, diameter (stem diameter outside bark measured at 4.5 feet to the last 0.1 inch), height (total tree height measured to the nearest foot), and tree location (determined through distance and azimuth measurements from a fixed point on the plot). Height was measured only on trees 5 inches or larger in diameter. Only measurements from live trees were considered.

On Forest Health Monitoring or Phase 3 (P3) plots, NRS FIA measures an additional suite of variables: soil characteristics, down woody material, understory vegetation, and crown characteristics. The SNF provided support to upgrade all Phase 2 (P2) plots to P3 plots in 2000 and 2001.

NRS FIA database tables were queried to obtain plot data within the three northeastern Minnesota counties (Cook, Lake, and St. Louis) that encompass the SNF. Phase 2 plots from 1999 to 2003 (MN cycle 12, subcycles 1-5) were queried. Because many of these plots are located outside the bounds of the SNF, BWCAW, and the 1999 blowdown, subsequent queries and analyses are constrained using geospatial overlays.

Table 10. Northern Forest Inventory and Analysis plot counts for the Boundary Waters Canoe Area Wilderness, 1999-2003.

Year	Cycle	Subcycle	P2	P3
1999	12	1	22	
2000	12	2	24	3
2001	12	3	0	55
2002	12	4	0	50
2003	12	5	54	3

Down Woody Material Sampling

Between 2001 and 2003, FIA sampled 317 P3 plots in forests of the Upper Great Lakes, with 89 plots in the BWCAW (34 in blowdown and 55 in nonblowdown areas) and 228 plots in the greater forest ecosystem outside the BWCAW (Ecoregion 212) (Fig. 19). We followed the down woody material sampling protocol detailed in Woodall and Williams (2005).

There were three study areas: (1) the greater forest ecosystem outside the BWCAW (Ecoregion 212), (2) inside the BWCAW in nonblowdown areas, and (3) inside the BWCAW in blowdown areas. Bailey (1995) delineated the forest ecosystem occupying the lake-swamp-morainic plains and lowlands of the Great Lakes and New England regions as the Laurentian Mixed Forest ecosystem (Ecoregion 212). In the Great Lakes area, the Ecoregion 212 stretches from the Canadian border in northwestern Minnesota across the northern areas of Wisconsin and Michigan (Fig. 32). All study plots were classified as inside or outside BWCAW blowdown areas by overlaying plot locations on coarse-scale sketch maps provided by the Minnesota Department of Natural Resources (Befort 2005).

Figure 32. Approximate plot locations (perturbed due to privacy laws) for study plots in the 212 ecosystem (gray area) and Boundary Waters Canoe Area Wilderness (boundary within inset). Data sources: National Atlas of the USA, ESRI Maps, and the USDA Forest Service.

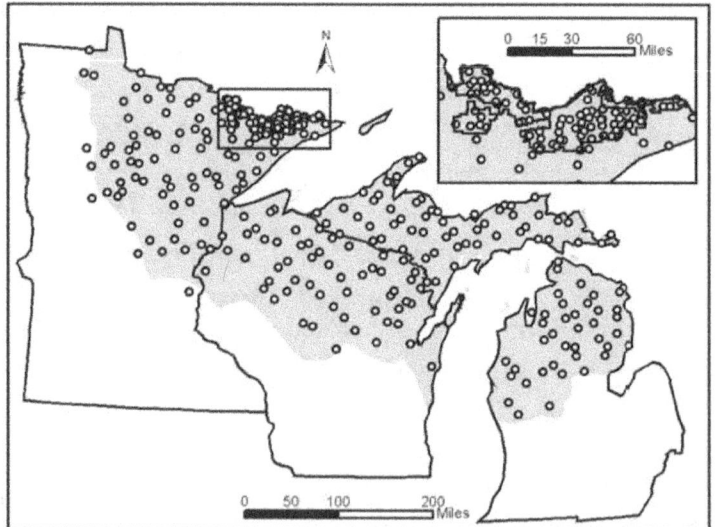

Geospatial Datasets and Analysis

Geographic information system (GIS) polygon delineations of the SNF, BWCAW, and the 1999 blowdown were obtained from the SNF. A 3-mile buffer surrounding blowdown polygons was created to identify the blowdown vicinity, within which some subsequent analyses were constrained. GIS layers of inventory plot center locations were created based on global positioning system (GPS) coordinates obtained during field data collection. The location of plots relative to geospatial datasets was determined via spatial join functions. Tabular attributes were added to NRS FIA plot tables, indicating whether each plot location occurred inside or outside each geographic area of interest (SNF,  BWCAW, blowdown polygon, 3-mile buffer). Subsequent tabular estimates of volume incorporated categorical attributes resulting from these spatial joins (Nelson and Moser 2007).

REFERENCES

Anderson, J.L.; Bell, J.C.; Cooper, T.H.; Grigal, D.F. 2001. Soils and landscapes of Minnesota. St. Paul, MN: University of Minnesota Extension Service. [Available online at: www.extension.umn.edu/distribution/cropsystems/DC2331.html]. Accessed 22 August 2006.

Ayres, H.B. 1899. Timber conditions of the pine region of Minnesota: Part I. Forest reserves. Washington, DC: U.S. Geological Survey, 21st Annual Report: 679-689.

Bailey, R.G. 1995. Description of the ecoregions of the United States. Misc. Publ. 1391. Washington, DC: U.S. Department of Agriculture, Forest Service.

Bechtold, W.A.; Patterson, P.L., eds. 2005. Forest Inventory and Analysis national sample design and estimation procedures. Gen. Tech. Rep. SRS-GTR-80. Asheville, NC: U.S. Department of Agriculture, Forest Service, Southern Research Station. 85 p.

Befort, B. 2005. Sketch map of BWCAW blowdown affected areas. St. Paul, MN: Minnesota Department of Natural Resources.

Bohlen, P.J.; Groffman, P.M.; Fahey, T.J.; Fisk, M.C.; Suarez, E.; Pelletier, D.M.; Fahey, R.T. 2004a. Ecosystem consequences of exotic earthworm invasion in north temperate forests. Ecosystems. 7(1): 1-12.

Bohlen, P.J.; Scheu, S.; Hale, C.M.; McLean, M.A.; Migge, S.; Groffman, P.M.; Parkinson, D. 2004b. Non-native invasive earthworms as agents of change in northern temperate forests. Frontiers in Ecology and Environment. 2(8): 427-435.

Brady, N.C. 1990. The nature and properties of soils. 10th ed. New York, NY: Macmillan. 639 p.

Canham, C.D.; Loucks, O.L. 1984. Catastrophic windthrow in the presettlement forests of Wisconsin. Ecology. 65: 803-809.

Frelich, L.E.; Graumlich, L.J. 1994. Age-class distribution and spatial patterns in an old-growth hemlock-hardwood forest. Canadian Journal of Forest Research. 24: 1939-1947.

Gundale, M.J. 2002. Influence of exotic earthworms on the soil organic horizon and the rare fern Botrychium mormo. Conservation Biology. 16(6): 1555-1561.

Hale, C.M.; Frelich, L.E.; Reich, P.B. 2005. Exotic European earthworm invasion dynamics in northern hardwood forests of Minnesota, USA. Ecological Applications. 15(3): 848-860.

Heinselman, M.L. 1973. Fire in the virgin forests of the Boundary Waters Canoe Area, Minnesota. Quaternary Research. 3: 329-382.

Heinselman, M.L. 1996. The Boundary Waters wilderness ecosystem. Minneapolis, MN: University of Minnesota Press.

Leuschen, T.; Wordell, T.; Finney, M.; Anderson, D.; Aunan, T.; Tine, P. 2000. Fuel risk assessment of the blowdown in the Boundary Waters Canoe Area Wilderness and adjacent lands. Duluth, MN: U.S. Department of Agriculture, Forest Service, Superior National Forest.

Magurran, A.E. 2003. Measuring biological diversity. Oxford: Blackwell.

Mattson, W.J.; Shriner, D.S., eds. 2001. Northern Minnesota Independence Day storm: a research needs assessment. Gen. Tech. Rep. NC-216. St. Paul, MN: U.S. Department of Agriculture, Forest Service, North Central Research Station. 65 p.

McWilliams, W.H.; O'Brien, R.A.; Reese, G.C.; Waddell, K.L. 2002. Distribution and abundance of oaks in North America. Chapter 2. In: McShea, W.J.; Healy, W.M., eds. The ecology and management of oaks for wildlife. [New York, NY]: Johns Hopkins Press: 13-33.

McBride, M.B. 1994. Environmental chemistry of soils. New York, NY: Oxford University Press. 406 p.

Miles, Patrick D.; Jacobson, Keith; Brand, Gary J.; Jepsen, Ed; Meneguzzo, Dacio; Mielke, Manfred E.; Olson, Cassandra; Perry, Charles H. (Hobie); Piva, Ron; Wilson, Barry Tyler; Woodall, Christopher. 2007. Minnesota's forests 1999-2003 (Part A). Resour. Bull. NRS-12A. Newtown Square, PA: U.S. Department of Agriculture, Forest Service, Northern Research Station. 92 p.

Nelson, M.D.; Moser, W.K. 2007. Integrating remote sensing and forest inventory data for assessing the BWCAC blowdown. In: Greer, J.D., ed. New remote sensing technologies for resource managers: procedings of the eleventh Forest Service remote sensing applications conference; 2006 April 24-28; Salt Lake City, UT. CD-ROM, American Society for Photogrammetry and Remote Sensing: 8 p.

O'Neill, K.P.; Amacher, M.C.; Perry, C.H. 2005. Soils as an indicator of forest health: a guide to the collection, analysis, and interpretation of soil indicator data in the Forest Inventory and Analysis program. Gen. Tech. Rep. NC-258. St. Paul, MN: U.S. Department of Agriculture, Forest Service, North Central Research Station. 53 p.

Peet, R.K. 1975. Relative diversity indices. Ecology 56(2): 496-498.

Peterson, C.J. 2000. Catastrophic wind damage to North American forests and the potential impact of climate change. Science of the Total Environment. 262: 287-311.

Pritchett, W.L.; Fisher, R.F. 1987. Properties and management of forest soils. 2d ed. New York, NY: John Wiley and Sons.

Spurr, S.H.; Barnes, B.V. 1980. Forest ecology. New York, NY: John Wiley and Sons. 687 p.

USDA, Forest Service. 2001. Final environmental impact statement for the Boundary Waters Canoe Area Wilderness fuel treatments. Milwaukee, WI: U.S. Department of Agriculture, Forest Service, Superior National Forest, Eastern Region. Vol. 1.

USDA, Forest Service. 2002. After the storm: a progress report, July 2002. Milwaukee, WI: U.S. Department of Agriculture, Forest Service, Superior National Forest, Eastern Region. [http://www.fs.fed.us/r9/forests/superior/storm_recovery/afterstorm/.] Accessed 6 April 2006.

USDA, Forest Service. 2006. History of the Boundary Waters Canoe Area Wilderness. Milwaukee, WI: U.S. Department of Agriculture, Forest Service, Superior National Forest, Eastern Region. [http://www.fs.fed.us/r9/forests/superior/bwcaw/bwhist.php.] Accessed 6 April 2006.

USDA, Natural Resources Conservation Service. 1999. Soil taxonomy: a basic system of soil classification for making and interpreting soil surveys. Agric. Handb. 436. Washington, DC: U.S. Department of Agriculture. 869 p.

Woodall, C.W.; Williams, M.S. 2005. Sample protocol, estimation procedures, and analytical guidelines for the down woody materials indicator of the FIA program. Gen. Tech. Rep. NC-256. St. Paul, MN: U.S. Department of Agriculture, Forest Service, North Central Research Station. 47 p.

Woods, K.D. 2004. Intermediate disturbance in a late-successional hemlock-northern hardwood forest. Journal of Ecology. 92: 464-476.

APPENDIX

Forest Inventory and Analysis defines forest land as treed land at least 1 acre in size, at least 120 feet in width, and possessing a minimum of 10-percent stocking of live trees. FIA separates forest land by two criteria: is the forest land productive or unproductive, and is the forest land reserved or unreserved? Combining these criteria, we define three components of forest land: (1) timberland—forest land that is not restricted from harvesting by statute, administrative regulation, or designation and is capable of growing trees at a rate of at least 20 cubic feet per acre per year at maximum annual increment; (2) reserved forest land—land that is restricted from harvesting by statute, administrative regulation, or designation (state and national parks, Federal wilderness areas, etc.); and (3) other forest land—low-productivity forest land that is not capable of growing trees at a rate of 20 cubic feet per acre per year. Because the Boundary Waters Canoe Area Wilderness has been designated as a wilderness area, all of the forest land within the BWCAW is considered to be reserved.

The FIA defines stand-size class as a function of the predominant (based on stocking) diameter class of live trees within the condition. Large-diameter trees are at least 11.0 inches in diameter for hardwoods and at least 9.0 inches in diameter for softwoods. Medium-diameter trees are at least 5.0 inches in diameter, but not as large as large-diameter trees. Small-diameter trees are less than 5.0 inches in diameter. A stand that is assigned to one of these three categories still might contain trees in one or both of the other two categories.